King Henry the 6th Part 2

By William Shakespeare

Edited by Julien Coallier

Copyright Julien Coallier 2012

All Rights Reserved.

Characters

Alexander Iden, a Kentish gentleman

All

Beadle

Bolingbroke, a conjurer

Both

Captain

Clerk of Chatham

Commons

Dick the Butcher, a follower of Cade

Duke of Buckingham

Duke of Gloucester, brother to the King

Duke/Earl of Somerset, John Beaufort

Earl of Salisbury

Earl of Suffolk

Earl of Warwick

Eleanor, duchess of Gloucester

Father John Hume, a priest

Father John Southwell, a priest

First 'Prentice

First Citizen

First Gentleman

First Murderer

First Neighbour

First Petitioner

George Bevis, a follower of Cade

Henry **VI**

Herald

Jack Cade, a rebel

John Holland, a follower of Cade

King Edward IV (Plantagenet)

Lord Clifford

Lord Say

Lord Scales

Margaret Jourdain, a witch

Master

Matthew Goffe

Mayor of Saint Alban's

Messenger

Michael, a follower of Cade

Peter, Thomas Horner's man

Post

Queen Margaret, daughter to Reignier, afterwards married to King Henry VI

Richard Plantagenet (Duke of Gloucester), becomes duke of York in Henry VI, Part

Richard Plantagenet the Younger

Second 'Prentice

Second Gentleman

Second Murderer

Second Neighbour

Second Petitioner

Servant

Servants

Sheriff

Simpcox, an imposter

Simpcox's Wife

Sir Humphrey Stafford, brother to William Stafford

Sir John Stanley

Smith the Weaver, a follower of Cade

Soldier

Spirit

Third Neighbour

Thomas Horner, an armourer

Townsman

Vaux

Walter Whitmore

William Stafford, brother to Sir Humphrey Stafford

Winchester, Henry Beaufort, great-uncle to Henry V, bishop of Winchster, and later cardinal

Young Clifford

Scenes

Act I - Page 13

Scene 1. London. The palace.

Scene 2. Gloucester's house.

Scene 3. The palace.

Scene 4. Gloucester's garden.

Act II - Page 62

Scene 1. Saint Alban's.

Scene 2. London. York's garden.

Scene 3. A hall of justice.

Scene 4. A street.

Act III - Page 105

Scene 1. The Abbey at Bury St. Edmund's.

Scene 2. Bury St. Edmund's. A room of state.

Scene 3. A bedchamber.

Act IV - Page 161

Scene 1. The coast of Kent.

Scene 2. Blackheath.

Scene 3. Another part of Blackheath.

Scene 4. London. The palace.

Scene 5. London. The Tower.

Scene 6. London. Cannon Street.

Scene 7. London. Smithfield.

Scene 8. Southwark.

Scene 9. Kenilworth Castle.

Scene 10. Kent. Iden's garden.

Act V - Page 225

Scene 1. Fields between Dartford and Blackheath.

Scene 2. Saint Alban's.

Scene 3. Fields near St. Alban's.

Act 1 Scene 1

London. The palace.

(Flourish) of trumpets:

King Henry VI, Gloucester, Salisbury, Warwick, and Cardinal, on the one side; Queen Margaret, Suffolk, York, Somerset, and Buckingham, on the other enter)

Suffolk

As by your high imperial majesty I had in charge at my depart for France, as procurator to your excellence, to marry Princess Margaret for your grace, so, in the famous ancient city, Tours, in presence of the Kings of France and Sicil, the Dukes of Orleans, Calaber, Bretagne and Alencon, seven earls, twelve barons and twenty reverend bishops, I have performed my task and was espoused

And humbly now upon my bended knee, in sight of England and her lordly peers deliver up my title in the queen to your most gracious hands, that are the substance of that great shadow I did represent

The happiest gift that ever marquess gave the fairest queen that ever king received.

King Henry VI

Suffolk, arise.

Welcome, Queen Margaret

I can express no kinder sign of love than this kind kiss.

Oh Lord, that lends me life, lend me a heart replete with thankfulness!

For thou hast given me in this beauteous face a world of earthly blessings to my soul, if sympathy of love unite our thoughts

Queen Margaret

Great King of England and my gracious lord, the mutual conference that my mind hath had, by day, by night, waking and in my dreams, in courtly company or at my beads with you, mine alder-liefest sovereign makes me the bolder to salute my king with ruder terms, such as my wit affords and over-joy of heart doth minister.

King Henry VI

Her sight did ravish

Her grace in speech, her words y-clad with wisdom's majesty, makes me from wondering fall to weeping joys

Such is the fulness of my heart's content.

Lords, with one cheerful voice welcome my love.

All

(Kneeling) Long live Queen Margaret, England's happiness!

Queen Margaret

We thank you all.

(Flourish)

Suffolk

My lord protector, so it please your grace, here are the articles of contracted peace between our sovereign and the French king Charles, or eighteen months concluded by consent.

Gloucester

(Reads) 'Imprimis, it is agreed between the French king Charles, and William de la Pole, Marquess of Suffolk, ambassador for Henry King of England, that the said Henry shall espouse the Lady Margaret, daughter unto Reignier King of Naples, Sicilia and Jerusalem, and crown her Queen of England were the thirtieth of May next ensuing item.

That the duchy of Anjou and the county of Maine shall be released and delivered to the king her father…

Let's the paper fall

King Henry VI

Uncle, how now!

Gloucester

Pardon me, gracious lord

Some sudden qualm hath struck me at the heart and dimmed mine eyes, that I can read no further.

King Henry VI

Uncle of Winchester, I pray, read on.

Cardinal

(Reads) It is further agreed between them, that the duchies of Anjou and Maine shall be released and delivered over to the king her father, and she sent over of the King of England's own proper cost and charges, without having any dowry.

King Henry VI

They please us well. Lord marquess, kneel down, we here create thee the first duke of Suffolk, and gird thee with the sword. Cousin of York, we here discharge your grace from being regent in the parts of France, till term of eighteen months be full expired.

Thanks, uncle Winchester, Gloucester, York, Buckingham, Somerset, Salisbury, and Warwick

We thank you all for the great favour done, in entertainment to my princely queen.

Come, let us in, and with all speed provide you see her coronation be performed.

(King Henry VI, Queen Margaret, and Suffolk exit)

Gloucester

Brave peers of England, pillars of the state, to you Duke Humphrey must unload his grief, your grief, the common grief of all the land.

What! did my brother Henry spend his youth, his valour, coin and people, in the wars?

Did he so often lodge in open field, in winter's cold and summer's parching heat to conquer France, his true inheritance?

And did my brother Bedford toil his wits, to keep by policy what Henry got?

Have you yourselves, Somerset, Buckingham, brave York, Salisbury, and victorious Warwick, received deep scars in France and Normandy?

Or hath mine uncle Beaufort and myself, with all the learned council of the realm, studied so long, sat in the council-house early and late, debating to and from

How France and Frenchmen might be kept in awe, and had his highness in his infancy crowned in Paris in despite of foes?

And shall these labours and these honours die?

Shall Henry's conquest, Bedford's vigilance, your deeds of war and all our counsel die?

Oh peers of England, shameful is this league!

Fatal this marriage, cancelling your fame, blotting your names from books of memory, razing the characters of your renown, defacing monuments of conquered France,

Undoing all, as all had never been!

Cardinal

Nephew, what means this passionate discourse, this peroration with such circumstance?

For France, it is ours

And we will keep it still.

Gloucester

Ay, uncle, we will keep it, if we can

But now it is impossible we should, Suffolk, the new-made duke that rules the roast hath given the duchy of Anjou and Maine unto the poor King Reignier, whose large style agrees not with the leanness of his purse.

Salisbury

Now, by the death of him that died for all, these counties were the keys of Normandy.

But wherefore weeps Warwick, my valiant son?

Warwick

For grief that they are past recovery, for, were there hope to conquer them again, my sword should shed hot blood, mine eyes no tears.

Anjou and Maine! myself did win them both

Those provinces these arms of mine did conquer, and are the cities, that I got with wounds delivered up again with peaceful words?

Mort Dieu!

York

For Suffolk's duke, may he be suffocate, that dims the honour of this warlike isle!

France should have torn and rent my very heart, before I would have yielded to this league.

I never read but England's kings have had large sums of gold and dowries with their wives, and our King Henry gives away his own, to match with her that brings no vantages.

Gloucester

A proper jest, and never heard before, that Suffolk should demand a whole fifteenth for costs and charges in transporting her!

She should have stayed in France and starved in France, Before…

Cardinal

My Lord of Gloucester, now ye grow too hot, it was the pleasure of my lord the King.

Gloucester

My Lord of Winchester, I know your mind

It is not my speeches that you do mislike, but it is my presence that doth trouble yee.

Rancour will out, proud prelate, in thy face I see thy fury if I longer stay, we shall begin our ancient bickerings.

Lordings, farewell

Say, when I am gone, I prophesied France will be lost here long.

(Exit)

Cardinal

So, there goes our protector in a rage.

It is known to you he is mine enemy, nay, more, an enemy unto you all, and no great friend, I fear me, to the king.

Consider, lords, he is the next of blood, and heir apparent to the English crown, had Henry got an empire by his marriage, and all the wealthy kingdoms of the west, there's reason he should be displeased at it.

Look to it, lords! Let not his smoothing words bewitch your hearts

Be wise and circumspect.

What though the common people favour him, calling him Humphrey, the good Duke of Gloucester, clapping their hands, and crying with loud voice, Jesus maintain your royal excellence!

With God preserve the good Duke Humphrey!

I fear me, lords, for all this flattering gloss, he will be found a dangerous protector.

Buckingham

Why should he, then, protect our sovereign, he being of age to govern of himself?

Cousin of Somerset, join you with me and all together, with the Duke of Suffolk, we'll quickly hoise Duke Humphrey from his seat.

Cardinal

This weighty business will not brook delay, I'll to the Duke of Suffolk presently.

(Exit)

Somerset

Cousin of Buckingham, though Humphrey's pride and greatness of his place be grief to us, yet let us watch the haughty cardinal, his insolence is more intolerable than all the princes in the land beside, if Gloucester be displaced, he'll be protector.

Buckingham

Or thou or I, Somerset, will be protector, despite Duke Humphrey or the cardinal.

(Buckingham and Somerset)

Salisbury

Pride went before, ambition follows him.

While these do labour for their own preferment, behoves it us to labour for the realm.

I never saw but Humphrey Duke of Gloucester did bear him like a noble gentleman.

Often have I seen the haughty cardinal, more like a soldier than a man of the church, as stout and proud as he were lord of all, swear like a ruffian and demean himself unlike the ruler of a commonweal.

Warwick, my son, the comfort of my age, thy deeds, thy plainness and thy housekeeping, hath won the greatest favour of the commons, excepting none but good Duke Humphrey

And brother York, thy acts in Ireland, in bringing them to civil discipline, thy late exploits done in the heart of France, when thou wert regent for our sovereign, have made thee feared and honoured of the people

Join we together, for the public good, in what we can, to bridle and suppress the pride of Suffolk and the cardinal, with Somerset's and Buckingham's ambition

And, as we may, cherish Duke Humphrey's deeds while they do tend the profit of the land.

Warwick

So God help Warwick, as he loves the land, and common profit of his country!

York

(From Aside) And so says York, for he hath greatest cause.

Salisbury

Then let's make haste away, and look unto the main.

Warwick

Unto the main! Oh father, Maine is lost

That Maine which by main force Warwick did win, and would have kept so long as breath did last!

Main chance, father, you meant; but I meant Maine, which I will win from France, or else be slain,

(Warwick and Salisbury exit)

York

Anjou and Maine are given to the French

Paris is lost

The state of Normandy stands on a tickle point, now they are gone, Suffolk concluded on the articles, the peers agreed, and Henry was well pleased to change two dukedoms for a duke's fair daughter.

I cannot blame them all: what is it to them?

It is thine they give away, and not their own.

Pirates may make cheap pennyworths of their pillage and purchase friends and give to courtezans, still revelling like lords till all be gone

While as the silly owner of the goods weeps over them and wrings his hapless hands and shakes his head and trembling stands aloof, while all is shared and all is borne away, ready to starve and dare not touch his own

So York must sit and fret and bite his tongue, while his own lands are bargain'd for and sold.

Methinks the realms of England, France and Ireland bear that proportion to my flesh and blood as did the fatal brand Althaea burned unto the prince's heart of Calydon.

Anjou and Maine both given unto the French!

Cold news for me, for I had hope of France, even as I have of fertile England's soil.

A day will come when York shall claim his own

And therefore I will take the Nevils' parts and make a show of love to proud Duke Humphrey, and when I spy advantage, claim the crown for that's the golden mark I seek to hit

Nor shall proud Lancaster usurp my right, nor hold the sceptre in his childish fist, nor wear the diadem upon his head, whose church-like humours fits not for a crown.

Then, York, be still awhile, till time do serve, watch thou and wake when others be asleep, to pry into the secrets of the state

Till Henry, surfeiting in joys of love, with his new bride and England's dear-bought queen, and Humphrey with the peers be fallen at jars

Then will I raise aloft the milk-white rose, with whose sweet smell the air shall be perfumed

And in my standard bear the arms of York to grapple with the house of Lancaster

Force perforce, I'll make him yield the crown, whose bookish rule hath pulled fair England down.

(Exit)

Act 1 Scene 2

Gloucester's house.

(Gloucester and his Duchess enter)

Duchess

Why droops my lord, like over-ripened corn, hanging the head at Ceres' plenteous load?

Why doth the great Duke Humphrey knit his brows, as frowning at the favours of the world?

Why are thine eyes fixed to the sullen earth, gazing on that which seems to dim thy sight?

What seest thou there? King Henry's diadem, enchased with all the honours of the world?

If so, gaze on, and grovel on thy face, until thy head be circled with the same.

Put forth thy hand, reach at the glorious gold.

What, is't too short? I'll lengthen it with mine, and having both together heaved it up, we'll both together lift our heads to heaven and never more abase our sight so low as to vouchsafe one glance unto the ground.

Gloucester

Oh Nell, sweet Nell, if thou dost love thy lord, banish the canker of ambitious thoughts.

And may that thought, when I imagine ill against my king and nephew, virtuous Henry, be my last breathing in this mortal world!

My troublous dream this night doth make me sad.

Duchess

What dreamed my lord? tell me, and I'll requite it with sweet rehearsal of my morning's dream.

Gloucester

Methought this staff, mine office-badge in court, was broke in twain; by whom I have forgot, but as I think, it was by the cardinal

On the pieces of the broken wand were placed the heads of Edmund Duke of Somerset, and William de la Pole, first duke of Suffolk.

This was my dream, what it doth bode, God knows.

Duchess

Tut, this was nothing but an argument that he that breaks a stick of Gloucester's grove shall lose his head for his presumption.

But list to me, my Humphrey, my sweet duke, methought I sat in seat of majesty in the cathedral church of Westminster, and in that chair where kings and queens are crowned

Where Henry and dame Margaret kneeled to me and on my head did set the diadem.

Gloucester

Nay, Eleanor, then must I chide outright, presumptuous dame, ill-nurtured Eleanor, art thou not second woman in the realm, and the protector's wife, beloved of him?

Hast thou not worldly pleasure at command, above the reach or compass of thy thought?

And wilt thou still be hammering treachery, to tumble down thy husband and thyself from top of honour to disgrace's feet?

Away from me, and let me hear no more!

Duchess

What, what, my lord! are you so choleric with Eleanor, for telling but her dream?

Next time I'll keep my dreams unto myself, and not be chequeed.

Gloucester

Nay, be not angry

I am pleased again.

(Messenger enters)

Messenger

My lord protector, it is his highness' pleasure you do prepare to ride unto Saint Alban's, where as the king and queen do mean to hawk.

Gloucester

I go.

Come, Nell, thou wilt ride with us?

Duchess

Yes, my good lord, I'll follow presently.

(Gloucester and Messenger exit)

Follow I must

I cannot go before, while Gloucester bears this base and humble mind.

Were I a man, a duke, and next of blood, I would remove these tedious stumbling-blocks and smooth my way upon their headless necks

Being a woman, I will not be slack to play my part in Fortune's pageant.

Where are you there? Sir John! nay, fear not, man, we are alone; here's none but thee and I.

(Hume enters)

Hume

Jesus preserve your royal majesty!

Duchess

What say'st thou? majesty! I am but grace.

Hume

But, by the grace of God, and Hume's advice, your grace's title shall be multiplied.

Duchess

What say'st thou, man? hast thou as yet conferred with Margery Jourdain, the cunning witch, with Roger Bolingbroke, the conjurer?

And will they undertake to do me good?

Hume

This they have promised, to show your highness a spirit raised from depth of under-ground, that shall make answer to such questions as by your grace shall be propounded him.

Duchess

It is enough

I'll think upon the questions, when from St. Alban's we do make return, we'll see these things effected to the full.

Here, Hume, take this reward

Make merry, man, with thy confederates in this weighty cause.

(Exit)

Hume

Hume must make merry with the duchess' gold

Marry, and shall.

But how now, Sir John Hume!

Seal up your lips, and give no words but mum, the business asketh silent secrecy.

Dame Eleanor gives gold to bring the witch, gold cannot come amiss, were she a devil.

Yet have I gold flies from another coast

I dare not say, from the rich cardinal and from the great and new-made Duke of Suffolk, yet I do find it so; for to be plain, they, knowing Dame Eleanor's aspiring humour have hired me to undermine the duchess and buz these conjurations in her brain.

They say a crafty knave does need no broker

Am I Suffolk and the cardinal's broker

Hume, if you take not heed, you shall go near to call them both a pair of crafty knaves.

Well, so it stands

Thus, I fear, at last Hume's knavery will be the duchess wreck, and her attainture will be Humphrey's fall, sort how it will, I shall have gold for all.

(Exit)

Act 1 Scene 3

The palace.

(Three or four Petitioners, Peter, the Armourer's man enter)

First Petitioner

My masters, let's stand close, my lord protector will come this way by and by, and then we may deliver our supplications in the quill.

Second Petitioner

Marry, the Lord protect him, for he's a good man!

Jesus bless him!

(Suffolk and Queen Margaret enter)

Peter

Here a' comes, methinks, and the queen with him.

I'll be the first, sure.

Second Petitioner

Come back, fool

This is the Duke of Suffolk, and not my lord protector.

Suffolk

How now, fellow! would'st anything with me?

First Petitioner

I pray, my lord, pardon me

I took ye for my lord protector.

Queen Margaret

(Reading) 'To my Lord Protector!' Are your

supplications to his lordship? Let me see them, what is thine?

First Petitioner

Mine is, and it please your grace, against John Goodman, my lord cardinal's man, for keeping my house, and lands, and wife and all, from me.

Suffolk

Thy wife, too! that's some wrong, indeed.

What's yours? What's here!

(Reads)

Against the Duke of Suffolk, for enclosing the commons of Melford.

How now, sir knave!

Second Petitioner

Alas, sir, I am but a poor petitioner of our whole township.

Peter

(Giving his petition) Against my master, Thomas Horner, for saying that the Duke of York was rightful heir to the crown.

Queen Margaret

What sayst thou? did the Duke of York say he was rightful heir to the crown?

Peter

That my master was?

No, forsooth, my master said that he was, and that the king was an usurper.

Suffolk

Who is there?

(Servant enter)

Take this fellow in, and send for his master with a pursuivant presently, we'll hear more of your matter before the King.

(Servant enters with Peter

Queen Margaret

And as for you, that love to be protected under the wings of our protector's grace, begin your suits anew, and sue to him.

Tears the supplication away, base cullions!

Suffolk, let them go.

All

Come, let's be gone.

(Exit)

Queen Margaret

My Lord of Suffolk, say, is this the guise, is this the fashion in the court of England?

Is this the government of Britain's isle, and this the royalty of Albion's king?

What shall King Henry be a pupil still under the surly Gloucester's governance?

Am I a queen in title and in style, and must be made a subject to a duke?

I tell thee, Pole, when in the city Tours thou ran'st a tilt in honour of my love and stolest away the ladies' hearts of France, I thought King Henry had resembled thee in courage, courtship and proportion, but all his mind is bent to holiness, to number Ave-Maries on his beads

His champions are the prophets and apostles, his weapons holy saws of sacred writ, his study is his tilt-yard, and his loves are brazen images of canonized saints.

I would the college of the cardinals would choose him pope, and carry him to Rome and set the triple crown upon his head, that were a state fit for his holiness.

Suffolk

Madam, be patient: as I was cause your highness came to England, so will I in England work your grace's full content.

Queen Margaret

Beside the haughty protector, have we Beaufort, the imperious churchman, Somerset, Buckingham, and grumbling York, and not the least of these but can do more in England than the king.

Suffolk

And he of these that can do most of all cannot do more in England than the Nevils, Salisbury and Warwick are no simple peers.

Queen Margaret

Not all these lords do vex me half so much as that proud dame, the lord protector's wife.

She sweeps it through the court with troops of ladies, more like an empress than Duke Humphrey's wife, strangers in court do take her for the queen

She bears a duke's revenues on her back and in her heart she scorns our poverty, shall I not live to be avenged on her?

Contemptuous base-born callet as she is, she vaunted amongst her minions to another day, the very train of her worst wearing gown was better worth than all my father's lands, till Suffolk gave two dukedoms for his daughter.

Suffolk

Madam, myself have limed a bush for her, and placed a quire of such enticing birds, that she will light to listen to the lays, and never mount to trouble you again.

So, let her rest, and madam, list to me

For I am bold to counsel you in this.

Although we fancy not the cardinal, yet must we join with him and with the lords, till we have brought Duke Humphrey in disgrace.

As for the Duke of York, this late complaint will make but little for his benefit.

So, one by one, we'll weed them all at last and you yourself shall steer the happy helm.

(Sound a sennet)

(King Henry VI, Gloucester, Cardinal, Buckingham, York, Somerset, Salisbury, Warwick, and the Duchess enter)

King Henry VI

For my part, noble lords, I care not which

Or Somerset or York, all's one to me.

York

If York have ill demeaned himself in France, then let him be denayed the regentship.

Somerset

If Somerset be unworthy of the place, let York be regent
I will yield to him.

Warwick

Whether your grace be worthy, yea or no, dispute not that, York is the worthier.

Cardinal

Ambitious Warwick, let thy betters speak.

Warwick

The cardinal's not my better in the field.

Buckingham

All in this presence are thy betters, Warwick.

Warwick

Warwick may live to be the best of all.

Salisbury

Peace, son! and show some reason, Buckingham, why Somerset should be preferred in this.

Queen Margaret

Because the king, forsooth, will have it so.

Gloucester

Madam, the king is old enough himself to give his censure: these are no women's matters.

Queen Margaret

If he be old enough, what needs your grace to be protector of his excellence?

Gloucester

Madam, I am protector of the realm

And, at his pleasure, will resign my place.

Suffolk

Resign it then and leave thine insolence.

Since thou wert king…

As who is king but thou?...

The commonwealth hath daily run to wreck

The Dauphin hath prevail'd beyond the seas

And all the peers and nobles of the realm have been as bondmen to thy sovereignty.

Cardinal

The commons hast thou rack'd; the clergy's bags are lank and lean with thy extortions.

Somerset

Thy sumptuous buildings and thy wife's attire have cost a mass of public treasury.

Buckingham

Thy cruelty in execution upon offenders, hath exceeded law, and left thee to the mercy of the law.

Queen Margaret

They sale of offices and towns in France, if they were known, as the suspect is great, would make thee quickly hop without thy head.

(Gloucester exits)

(Queen Margaret drops her fan)

Give me my fan: what, minion! can ye not?

(She gives the Duchess a box on the ear)

I cry you mercy, madam

Was it you?

Duchess

Was it I! yea, I it was, proud Frenchwoman, could I come near your beauty with my nails, I'd set my ten commandments in your face.

King Henry VI

Sweet aunt, be quiet

It was against her will.

Duchess

Against her will! good king, look to it in time

She'll hamper thee, and dandle thee like a baby, though in this place most master wear no breeches. she shall not strike Dame Eleanor unrevenged.

(Exit)

Buckingham

Lord cardinal, I will follow Eleanor, and listen after Humphrey, how he proceeds

She's tickled now, her fume needs no spurs, she'll gallop far enough to her destruction.

(Exit)

(Gloucester re-enters)

Gloucester

Now, lords, my choler being over-blown with walking once about the quadrangle, I come to talk of commonwealth affairs.

As for your spiteful false objections, prove them, and I lie open to the law, but God in mercy so deal with my soul as I in duty love my king and country!

But, to the matter that we have in hand, I say, my sovereign, York is meetest man to be your regent in the realm of France.

Suffolk

Before we make election, give me leave to show some reason, of no little force, that York is most unmeet of any man.

York

I'll tell thee, Suffolk, why I am unmeet, first, for I cannot flatter thee in pride

Next, if I be appointed for the place, my Lord of Somerset will keep me here, without discharge, money, or furniture till France be won into the Dauphin's hands

Last time, I danced attendance on his will till Paris was besieged, famished and lost.

Warwick

That can I witness; and a fouler fact did never traitor in the land commit.

Suffolk

Peace, headstrong Warwick!

Warwick

Image of pride, why should I hold my peace?

(Horner, the Armourer, and his man Peter enter guarded)

Suffolk

Because here is a man accused of treason, pray God the Duke of York excuse himself!

York

Doth any one accuse York for a traitor?

King Henry VI

What mean'st thou, Suffolk; tell me, what are these?

Suffolk

Please it your majesty, this is the man that doth accuse his master of high treason, his words were these: that Richard, Duke of York, was rightful heir unto the English crown and that your majesty was a usurper.

King Henry VI

Say, man, were these thy words?

Horner

And it shall please your majesty, I never said nor thought any such matter, God is my witness, I am falsely accused by the villain.

Peter

By these ten bones, my lords, he did speak them to me in the garret one night, as we were scouring my Lord of York's armour.

York

Base dunghill villain and mechanical, I'll have thy head for this thy traitor's speech.

I do beseech your royal majesty, let him have all the rigor of the law.

Horner

Alas, my lord, hang me, if ever I spake the words.

My accuser is my apprentice

And when I did correct him for his fault the other day, he did vow upon his knees he would be even with me, I have good witness of this: therefore I beseech your majesty, do not cast away an honest man for a villain's accusation.

King Henry VI

Uncle, what shall we say to this in law?

Gloucester

This doom, my lord, if I may judge, let Somerset be regent over the French, because in York this breeds suspicion

Let these have a day appointed them for single combat in convenient place, for he hath witness of his servant's malice

This is the law, and this Duke Humphrey's doom.

Somerset

I humbly thank your royal majesty.

Horner

And I accept the combat willingly.

Peter

Alas, my lord, I cannot fight

For God's sake, pity my case.

The spite of man prevaileth against me.

Oh Lord, have mercy upon me!

I shall never be able to fight a blow.

Oh Lord, my heart!

Gloucester

Sirrah, or you must fight, or else be hanged.

King Henry VI

Away with them to prison; and the day of combat shall be the last of the next month.

Come, Somerset, we'll see thee sent away.

(Flourish)

(Exit)

Act 1 Scene 4

Gloucester's garden.

(Margaret Jourdain, Hume, Southwell, and Bolingbroke enter)

Hume

Come, my masters; the duchess, I tell you, expects performance of your promises.

Bolingbroke

Master Hume, we are therefore provided, will her ladyship behold and hear our exorcisms?

Hume

Ay, what else? fear you not her courage.

Bolingbroke

I have heard her reported to be a woman of an invincible spirit, but it shall be convenient, Master Hume, that you be by her aloft, while we be busy below

So, I pray you, go, in God's name, and leave us.

(Hume exists)

Mother Jourdain, be you prostrate and grovel on the earth

John Southwell, read you

Let us to our work.

The Duchess enters aloft, Hume following)

Duchess

Well said, my masters

Welcome all.

To this gear the sooner the better.

Bolingbroke

Patience, good lady

Wizards know their times, deep night, dark night, the silent of the night, the time of night when Troy was set on fire

The time when screech-owls cry and ban-dogs howl, and spirits walk and ghosts break up their graves, that time best fits the work we have in hand.

Madam, sit you and fear not, whom we raise, we will make fast within a hallowed verge.

Here they do the ceremonies belonging, and make the circle

(Bolingbroke or Southwell reads: I summon thee spirit, arise now, hear us, spirit I seek you forth)

(It thunders and lightens terribly, then the Spirit rises)

Spirit

Adsum

Margaret Jourdain

Asmath, by the eternal God, whose name and power thou tremblest at, answer that I shall ask

For, till thou speak, thou shalt not pass from hence.

Spirit

Ask what thou wilt. That I had said and done!

Bolingbroke

First of the king: what shall of him become?'

(Reading out of a paper)

Spirit

The duke yet lives that Henry shall depose

But him outlive, and die a violent death.

As the Spirit speaks, Southwell writes the answer

Bolingbroke

What fates await the Duke of Suffolk?

Spirit

By water shall he die, and take his end.

Bolingbroke

What shall befall the Duke of Somerset?

Spirit

Let him shun castles

Safer shall he be upon the sandy plains than where castles mounted stand.

Have done, for more I hardly can endure.

Bolingbroke

Descend to darkness and the burning lake!

False fiend, avoid!

(Thunder and lightning

(Spirit exits)

(York and Buckingham enter with their Guard and break in)

York

Lay hands upon these traitors and their trash.

Beldam, I think we watched you at an inch.

What, madam, are you there?

The king and commonweal are deeply indebted for this piece of pains, my lord protector will, I doubt it not

See you well guerdon'd for these good deserts.

Duchess

Not half so bad as thine to England's king,

Injurious duke, that threatest where's no cause.

Buckingham

True, madam, none at all, what call you this?

Away with them! let them be clapped up close.

And kept asunder.

You, madam, shall with us.

Stafford, take her to thee.

(Exit)

(Above Duchess and Hume, guarded)

We'll see your trinkets here all forthcoming.

All, away!

(Guard exits with Margaret Jourdain, Southwell)

York

Lord Buckingham, methinks, you watched her well, a pretty plot, well chosen to build upon!

Now, pray, my lord, let's see the devil's writ.

What have we here?

(Reads)

Of the duke yet lives, that Henry shall depose

But him out live and die a violent death.

Why, this is just…

I say, Aeacides, that the Romans can defeat you, well, to the rest, tell me what fate awaits the Duke of Suffolk?

By water shall he die, and take his end.

What shall betide the Duke of Somerset?

Let him shun castles

Safer shall he be upon the sandy plains than where castles mounted stand.

Come, come, my lords

These oracles are hardly attained, and hardly understood.

The king is now in progress towards Saint Alban's, with him the husband of this lovely lady, thither go these news, as fast as horse can carry them, a sorry breakfast for my lord protector.

Buckingham

Your grace shall give me leave, my Lord of York, to be the post, in hope of his reward.

York

At your pleasure, my good lord.

Who's within there, ho!

(A Servingman enters)

Invite my Lords of Salisbury and Warwick to supper with me tomorrow night.

Away!

(Exit)

Act 2 Scene 1

Saint Alban's.

(King Henry VI, Queen Margaret, Gloucester, Cardinal, and Suffolk enter, with Falconers)

Queen Margaret

Believe me, lords, for flying at the brook, I saw not better sport these seven years' day, yet, by your leave, the wind was very high

Ten to one, old Joan had not gone out.

King Henry VI

But what a point, my lord, your falcon made, and what a pitch she flew above the rest!

To see how God in all his creatures works!

Yea, man and birds are fain of climbing high.

Suffolk

No marvel, and it like your majesty, my lord protector's hawks do tower so well

They know their master loves to be aloft and bears his thoughts above his falcon's pitch.

Gloucester

My lord, it is but a base ignoble mind that mounts no higher than a bird can soar.

Cardinal

I thought as much; he would be above the clouds.

Gloucester

Ay, my lord cardinal? how think you by that?

Were it not good your grace could fly to heaven?

King Henry VI

The treasury of everlasting joy.

Cardinal

Thy heaven is on earth; thine eyes and thoughts beat on a crown, the treasure of thy heart

Pernicious protector, dangerous peer, that smooth'st it so with king and commonweal!

Gloucester

What, cardinal, is your priesthood grown peremptory?

Is there so much anger in the minds of the gods?

Churchmen so hot? good uncle, hide such malice

With such holiness can you do it?

Suffolk

No malice, sir

No more than well becomes so good a quarrel and so bad a peer.

Gloucester

As who, my lord?

Suffolk

Why, as you, my lord,

And is it like your lordly lord-protectorship.

Gloucester

Why, Suffolk, England knows thine insolence.

Queen Margaret

And thy ambition, Gloucester.

King Henry VI

I pray to thee, peace, good queen, and whet not on these furious peers

For blessed are the peacemakers on earth.

Cardinal

Let me be blessed for the peace I make, against this proud protector, with my sword!

Gloucester

(*From aside to Cardinal*) Faith, holy uncle, would it were come to that!

Cardinal

(*From aside to Gloucester*) Marry, when thou darest.

Gloucester

(From aside to Cardinal) Make up no factious numbers for the matter

In thine own person answer thy abuse.

Cardinal

(From aside to Gloucester) Ay, where thou darest not peep, an if thou darest, this evening, on the east side of the grove.

King Henry VI

How now, my lords!

Cardinal

Believe me, cousin Gloucester, had not your man put up the fowl so suddenly, we had had more sport.

(From aside to Gloucester)

Come with thy two-hand sword.

Gloucester

True, uncle.

Cardinal

(From aside to Gloucester) Are ye advised?

The east side of the grove?

Gloucester

(From aside to Cardinal) Cardinal, I am with you.

King Henry VI

Why, how now, uncle Gloucester!

Gloucester

Talking of hawking; nothing else, my lord.

(From aside to Cardinal)

Now, by God's mother, priest, I'll shave your crown for this, or all my fence shall fail.

Cardinal

(From aside to Gloucester) Medice, teipsum--

Protector, see to it well, protect yourself.

King Henry VI

The winds grow high

So do your stomachs, lords.

How irksome is this music to my heart!

When such strings jar, what hope of harmony?

I pray, my lords, let me compound this strife.

(A Townsman of Saint Alban's enters, crying: A miracle!)

Gloucester

What means this noise?

Fellow, what miracle dost thou proclaim?

Townsman

A miracle! a miracle!

Suffolk

Come to the king and tell him what miracle.

Townsman

Forsooth, a blind man at Saint Alban's shrine, within this half-hour, hath received his sight

A man that never saw in his life before.

King Henry VI

Now, God be praised, that to believing souls gives light in darkness, comfort in despair!

The Mayor of Saint Alban's and his brethren enter, bearing Simpcox, between two in a chair, Simpcox's Wife following)

Cardinal

Here comes the townsmen on procession, to present your highness with the man.

King Henry VI

Great is his comfort in this earthly vale, although by his sight his sin be multiplied.

Gloucester

Stand by, my masters, bring him near the king

His highness' pleasure is to talk with him.

King Henry VI

Good fellow, tell us here the circumstance, that we for thee may glorify the Lord.

What, hast thou been long blind and now restored?

Simpcox

Born blind, and it please your grace.

Wife

Ay, indeed, was he.

Suffolk

What woman is this?

Wife

His wife, and it like your worship.

Gloucester

Hadst thou been his mother, thou couldst have better told.

King Henry VI

Where wert thou born?

Simpcox

At Berwick in the north, and it like your grace.

King Henry VI

Poor soul, God's goodness hath been great to thee

Let never day nor night unhallowed pass, but still remember what the Lord hath done.

Queen Margaret

Tell me, good fellow, camest thou here by chance, or of devotion, to this holy shrine?

Simpcox

God knows, of pure devotion; being called a hundred times and oftener, in my sleep, by good Saint Alban

Who said, Simpcox come, come, offer at my shrine and I will help thee.

Wife

Most true, forsooth

Many time and often myself have heard a voice to call him so.

Cardinal

What, art thou lame?

Simpcox

Ay, God Almighty help me!

Suffolk

How camest thou so?

Simpcox

A fall off of a tree.

Wife

A plum-tree, master.

Gloucester

How long hast thou been blind?

Simpcox

Born so, master.

Gloucester

What, and wouldst climb a tree?

Simpcox

But that in all my life, when I was a youth.

Wife

Too true

And bought his climbing very dear.

Gloucester

Mass, thou lovedst plums well, that wouldst venture so.

Simpcox

Alas, good master, my wife desired some damsons, and made me climb, with danger of my life.

Gloucester

A subtle knave! but yet it shall not serve.

Let me see thine eyes: wink now: now open them, in my opinion yet thou seest not well.

Simpcox

Yes, master, clear as day, I thank God and Saint Alban.

Gloucester

Say'st thou me so? What colour is this cloak of?

Simpcox

Red, master

Red as blood.

Gloucester

Why, that's well said.

What colour is my gown of?

Simpcox

Black, forsooth, coal-black as jet.

King Henry VI

Why, then, thou know'st what colour jet is of?

Suffolk

And yet, I think, jet did he never see.

Gloucester

But cloaks and gowns, before this day, a many.

Wife

Never before this day, in all his life.

Gloucester

Tell me, sirrah, what's my name?

Simpcox

Alas, master, I know not.

Gloucester

What's his name?

Simpcox

I know not.

Gloucester

Nor his?

Simpcox

No, indeed, master.

Gloucester

What's thine own name?

Simpcox

Saunder Simpcox, and if it please you, master.

Gloucester

Then, Saunder, sit there, the lyingest knave in Christendom.

If thou hadst been born blind, thou mightest as well have known all our names as thus to name the several colours we do wear.

Sight may distinguish of colours, but suddenly to nominate them all, it is impossible.

My lords, Saint Alban here hath done a miracle

Would ye not think his cunning to be great, that could restore this cripple to his legs again?

Simpcox

Oh master, that you could!

Gloucester

My masters of Saint Alban's, have you not beadles in your town, and things called whips?

Mayor

Yes, my lord, if it please your grace.

Gloucester

Then send for one presently.

Mayor

Sirrah, go fetch the beadle hither straight.

(An Attendant exits)

Gloucester

Now fetch me a stool hither by and by.

Now, sirrah, if you mean to save yourself from whipping, leap me over this stool and run away.

Simpcox

Alas, master, I am not able to stand alone

You go about to torture me in vain.

(A Beadle enters with whips)

Gloucester

Well, sir, we must have you find your legs.

Sirrah beadle, whip him till he leap over that same stool.

Beadle

I will, my lord.

Come on, sirrah

Off with your doublet quickly.

Simpcox

Alas, master, what shall I do?

I am not able to stand.

(After the Beadle hits him once, he leaps over the stool and runs away, they follow and cry, 'A miracle!')

King Henry VI

Oh God, seest Thou this, and bearest so long?

Queen Margaret

It made me laugh to see the villain run.

Gloucester

Follow the knave; and take this drab away.

Wife

Alas, sir, we did it for pure need.

Gloucester

Let them be whipped through every market-town, till they come to Berwick, from whence they came.

(Wife, Beadle, Mayor exit)

Cardinal

Duke Humphrey has done a miracle to-day.

Suffolk

True

Made the lame to leap and fly away.

Gloucester

But you have done more miracles than I

You made in a day, my lord, whole towns to fly.

(Buckingham enters)

King Henry VI

What tidings with our cousin Buckingham?

Buckingham

Such as my heart doth tremble to unfold.

A sort of naughty persons, lewdly bent under the countenance and confederacy of Lady Eleanor, the protector's wife

The ringleader and head of all this rout have practised dangerously against your state, dealing with witches and with conjurers

Whom we have apprehended in the fact

Raising up wicked spirits from under ground, demanding of King Henry's life and death, and other of your highness' privy-council

As more at large your grace shall understand.

Cardinal

(From aside to Gloucester) And so, my lord protector, by this means your lady is forthcoming yet at London.

This news, I think, hath turned your weapon's edge

It is like, my lord, you will not keep your hour.

Gloucester

Ambitious churchman, leave to afflict my heart

Sorrow and grief have vanquish'd all my powers

And, vanquished as I am, I yield to thee, or to the meanest groom.

King Henry VI

Oh God, what mischiefs work the wicked ones, heaping confusion on their own heads thereby!

Queen Margaret

Gloucester, see here the tainture of thy nest.

And look thyself be faultless, thou wert best.

Gloucester

Madam, for myself, to heaven I do appeal, how I have loved my king and commonweal, and for my wife I know not how it stands

Sorry I am to hear what I have heard, noble she is but if she have forgot honour and virtue and conversed with such as like to pitch defile nobility, I banish her my bed and company, and give her as a prey to law and shame that hath dishonoured Gloucester's honest name.

King Henry VI

Well, for this night we will repose us here, to-morrow toward London back again to look into this business thoroughly and call these foul offenders to their answers and poise the cause in justice' equal scales whose beam stands sure, whose rightful cause prevails.

(Flourish)

(Exit)

Act 2 Scene 2

London. York's garden.

(York, Salisbury, and Warwick enter)

York

Now, my good Lords of Salisbury and Warwick, our simple supper ended, give me leave in this close walk to satisfy myself in craving your opinion of my title, which is infallible to England's crown.

Salisbury

My lord, I long to hear it at full.

Warwick

Sweet York, begin: and if thy claim be good, the Nevils are thy subjects to command.

York

Then thus, Edward the Third, my lords, had seven sons, the first, Edward the Black Prince, Prince of Wales

The second, William of Hatfield, and the third, Lionel Duke of Clarence, next to whom was John of Gaunt, the Duke of Lancaster

The fifth was Edmund Langley, Duke of York

The sixth was Thomas of Woodstock, Duke of Gloucester

William of Windsor was the seventh and last.

Edward the Black Prince died before his father and left behind him Richard, his only son, who after Edward the Third's death reigned as king

Till Henry Bolingbroke, Duke of Lancaster, the eldest son and heir of John of Gaunt, crowned by the name of Henry the Fourth, seized on the realm, deposed the rightful king, sent his poor queen to France from whence she came, and him to Pomfret

Where, as all you know, harmless Richard was murdered traitorously.

Warwick

Father, the duke hath told the truth, thus got the house of Lancaster the crown.

York

Which now they hold by force and not by right

For Richard, the first son's heir, being dead, the issue of the next son should have reigned.

Salisbury

But William of Hatfield died without an heir.

York

The third son, Duke of Clarence, from whose line I claimed the crown, had issue, Philippe, a daughter

Who married Edmund Mortimer, Earl of March, Edmund had issue, Roger Earl of March

Roger had issue, Edmund, Anne and Eleanor.

Salisbury

This Edmund, in the reign of Bolingbroke, as I have read, laid claim unto the crown

But for Owen Glendower, had been king, who kept him in captivity till he died.

But to the rest.

York

His eldest sister, Anne, my mother, being heir unto the crown married Richard Earl of Cambridge

Who was son to Edmund Langley, Edward the Third's fifth son.

By her I claim the kingdom, she was heir to Roger Earl of March, who was the son of Edmund Mortimer, who married Philippe, sole daughter unto Lionel Duke of Clarence

So, if the issue of the elder son

Succeed before the younger, I am king.

Warwick

What plain proceeding is more plain than this?

Henry doth claim the crown from John of Gaunt, the fourth son

York claims it from the third.

Till Lionel's issue fails, his should not reign, it fails not yet, but flourishes in thee and in thy sons, fair slips of such a stock.

Then, father Salisbury, kneel we together

In this private plot be we the first that shall salute our rightful sovereign with honour of his birthright to the crown.

Both

Long live our sovereign Richard, England's king!

York

We thank you, lords.

But I am not your king till I be crowned and that my sword be stained with heart-blood of the house of Lancaster

And that's not suddenly to be performed, but with advice and silent secrecy.

Do you as I do in these dangerous days, wink at the Duke of Suffolk's insolence, at Beaufort's pride, at Somerset's ambition, at Buckingham and all the crew of them till they have snared the shepherd of the flock, that virtuous prince, the good Duke Humphrey

It is that they seek, and they in seeking that shall find their deaths, if York can prophesy.

Salisbury

My lord, break we off

We know your mind at full.

Warwick

My heart assures me that the Earl of Warwick shall one day make the Duke of York a king.

York

And, Nevil, this I do assure myself

Richard shall live to make the Earl of Warwick the greatest man in England but the king.

(Exit)

Act 2 Scene 3

A hall of justice.

(trumpets sound)

(King Henry VI, Queen Margaret, Gloucester, York, Suffolk, and Salisbury; the Duchess, Margaret Jourdain, Southwell, Hume, and Bolingbroke enter, under guard)

King Henry VI

Stand forth, Dame Eleanor Cobham, Gloucester's wife, in sight of God and us, your guilt is great.

Receive the sentence of the law for sins, such as by God's book are adjudged to death.

You four, from hence to prison back again

From thence unto the place of execution, the witch in Smithfield shall be burned to ashes, and you three shall be strangled on the gallows.

You, madam, for you are more nobly born, despoiled of your honour in your life, shall, after three days' open penance done, live in your country here in banishment with Sir John Stanley, in the Isle of Man.

Duchess

Welcome is banishment

Welcome were my death.

Gloucester

Eleanor, the law, thou see'st, hath judged thee, I cannot justify whom the law condemns.

(Duchess and other prisoners exit, guarded)

Mine eyes are full of tears, my heart of grief.

Ah, Humphrey, this dishonour in thine age will bring thy head with sorrow to the ground!

I beseech your majesty, give me leave to go

Sorrow would solace and mine age would ease.

King Henry VI

Stay, Humphrey Duke of Gloucester, here thou go, give up thy staff, Henry will to himself protector be

God shall be my hope, my stay, my guide and lantern to my feet, and go in peace, Humphrey, no less beloved than when thou wert protector to thy King.

Queen Margaret

I see no reason why a king of years should be to be protected like a child.

God and King Henry govern England's realm.

Give up your staff, sir, and the king his realm.

Gloucester

My staff? here, noble Henry, is my staff

As willingly do I the same resign as ever thy father Henry made it mine

And even as willingly at thy feet I leave it as others would ambitiously receive it.

Farewell, good king, when I am dead and gone, may honourable peace attend thy throne!

(Exit)

Queen Margaret

Why, now is Henry king, and Margaret queen

And Humphrey Duke of Gloucester scarce himself, that bears so shrewd a maim

Two pulls at once

His lady banished, and a limb lopp'd off.

This staff of honour raught, there let it stand where it best fits to be, in Henry's hand.

Suffolk

Thus droops this lofty pine and hangs his sprays

Thus Eleanor's pride dies in her youngest days.

York

Lords, let him go.

Please it your majesty, this is the day appointed for the combat

And ready are the appellant and defendant, the armourer and his man to enter the lists, so please your highness to behold the fight.

Queen Margaret

Ay, good my lord

For purposely therefore left I the court, to see this quarrel tried.

King Henry VI

Oh God's name, see the lists and all things fit, here let them end it; and God defend the right!

York

I never saw a fellow worse bested, or more afraid to fight, than is the appellant, the servant of this armourer, my lords.

(Horner, the Armourer, and his Neighbours enter at one door, drinking to him so much that he is drunk. Horner enters with a drum before him and his staff with a sand-bag fastened to it)

(At the other door Peter enters, his man, with a drum and sand-bag, and apprentices drinking to him)

First Neighbour

Here, neighbour Horner, I drink to you in a cup of sack, and fear not, neighbour, you shall do well enough.

Second Neighbour

And here, neighbour, here's a cup of charneco.

Third Neighbour

And here's a pot of good double beer, neighbor, drink, and fear not your man.

Horner

Let it come, in faith, and I'll pledge you all a fig for Peter!

First apprentice here, Peter, I drink to thee, and be not afraid.

Second apprentice

Be merry, Peter, and fear not thy master, fight for credit of the apprentices.

Peter

I thank you all, drink, and pray for me, I pray you

For I think I have taken my last draught in this world.

Here, Robin, an if I die, I give thee my apron, and will, thou shalt have my hammer, and here, Tom, take all the money that I have.

Oh Lord bless me! I pray God! for I am never able to

deal with my master, he hath learnt me so much fence already.

Salisbury

Come, leave your drinking, and fall to blows.

Sirrah, what's thy name?

Peter

Peter, forsooth.

Salisbury

Peter! what more?

Peter

Thump.

Salisbury

Thump! then see thou thump thy master well.

Horner

Masters, I am come hither, as it were, upon my man's instigation, to prove him a knave and myself an honest man

Touching the Duke of York, I will take my death, I never meant him any ill, nor the king, nor the queen, and therefore Peter have at thee with a downright blow!

York

Dispatch, this knave's tongue begins to double.

Sound, trumpets, alarum to the combatants!

Alarum.

(They fight, and Peter strikes him down)

Horner

Hold, Peter, hold! I confess, I confess treason.

(Dies)

York

Take away his weapon.

Fellow, thank God, and the good wine in thy master's way.

Peter

Oh God, have I overcome mine enemy in this presence?

Oh Peter, thou hast prevailed in right!

King Henry VI

Go, take hence that traitor from our sight

For his death we do perceive his guilt, and God in justice hath revealed to us the truth and innocence of this poor fellow, which he had thought to have murdered wrongfully.

Come, fellow, follow us for thy reward.

Sound a flourish.

(Flourish)

(Exit)

Act 2 Scene 4

A street.

(Gloucester and his Servingmen enter in mourning cloaks)

Gloucester

Thus sometimes hath the brightest day a cloud

And after summer evermore succeeds Barren winter, with his wrathful nipping cold, so cares and joys abound, as seasons fleet.

Sirs, what's o'clock?

Servants

Ten, my lord.

Gloucester

Ten is the hour that was appointed me to watch the coming of my punish'd duchess, uneath may she endure the flinty streets to tread them with her tender-feeling feet.

Sweet Nell, ill can thy noble mind abrook the abject people gazing on thy face, with envious looks, laughing at thy shame, that did follow thy proud chariot-wheels when thou didst ride in triumph through the streets.

But, soft! I think she comes

I'll prepare my tear-stained eyes to see her miseries.

(The Duchess enters in a white sheet, and a taper burning in her hand, with Stanley, the Sheriff, and Officers)

Servant

So please your grace, we'll take her from the sheriff.

Gloucester

No, stir not, for your lives; let her pass by.

Duchess

Come you, my lord, to see my open shame?

Now thou dost penance too. Look how they gaze!

See how the giddy multitude do point, and nod their heads, and throw their eyes on thee!

Ah, Gloucester, hide thee from their hateful looks, and, in thy closet pent up, rue my shame, and ban thine enemies, both mine and thine!

Gloucester

Be patient, gentle Nell; forget this grief.

Duchess

Ah, Gloucester, teach me to forget myself!

For whilst I think I am thy married wife and thou a prince, protector of this land, methinks I should not thus be led along, mailed up in shame, with papers on my back, and followed with a rabble that rejoice to see my tears and hear my deep-fet groans.

The ruthless flint doth cut my tender feet, and when I start, the envious people laugh and bid me be advised how I tread.

Ah, Humphrey, can I bear this shameful yoke?

Trow'st thou that ever I'll look upon the world, or count them happy that enjoy the sun?

No

Dark shall be my light and night my day

To think upon my pomp shall be my hell

Sometime I'll say, I am Duke Humphrey's wife, and he a prince and ruler of the land, yet so he ruled and such a prince he was as he stood by whilst I, his forlorn duchess, was made a wonder and a pointing-stock to every idle rascal follower.

But be thou mild and blush not at my shame, nor stir at nothing till the axe of death hang over thee, as sure it shortly will

For Suffolk, he that can do all in all with her that hateth thee and hates us all, and York and impious Beaufort, that false priest have all limed bushes to betray thy wings, and, fly thou how thou canst they'll tangle thee

But fear not thou, until thy foot be snared, nor never seek prevention of thy foes.

Gloucester

Ah, Nell, forbear! thou aimest all awry

I must offend before I be attainted

And had I twenty times so many foes, and each of them had twenty times their power, all these could not procure me any scathe, so long as I am loyal, true and crimeless.

Wouldst have me rescue thee from this reproach?

Why, yet thy scandal were not wiped away but I in danger for the breach of law.

Thy greatest help is quiet, gentle Nell, I pray thee, sort thy heart to patience

These few days' wonder will be quickly worn.

(A Herald enters)

Herald

I summon your grace to his majesty's parliament, Holden at Bury the first of this next month.

Gloucester

And my consent ne'er asked herein before!

This is close dealing.

Well, I will be there.

(Herald exits)

My Nell, I take my leave: and, master sheriff, let not her penance exceed the king's commission.

Sheriff

And if it please your grace, here my commission stays, and Sir John Stanley is appointed now yo take her with him to the Isle of Man.

Gloucester

Must you, Sir John, protect my lady here?

Stanley

So am I given in charge, may it please your grace.

Gloucester

Entreat her not the worse in that I pray you use her well, the world may laugh again

I may live to do you kindness if you do it her, and so sir John, farewell!

Duchess

What, gone, my lord, and bid me not farewell!

Gloucester

Witness my tears, I cannot stay to speak.

(Gloucester and Servingmen exit)

Duchess

Art thou gone too? all comfort go with thee!

For none abides with me: my joy is death

Death, at whose name I often have been afear'd because I wished this world's eternity.

Stanley, I pray to thee, go, and take me hence

I care not whither, for I beg no favour, only convey me where thou art commanded.

Stanley

Why, madam, that is to the Isle of Man

There to be used according to your state.

Duchess

That's bad enough, for I am but reproach, and shall I then be used reproachfully?

Stanley

Like to a duchess, and Duke Humphrey's lady

According to that state you shall be used.

Duchess

Sheriff, farewell, and better than I fare, although thou hast been conduct of my shame

Sheriff

It is my office

Madam, pardon me.

Duchess

Ay, ay, farewell

Thy office is discharged.

Come, Stanley, shall we go?

Stanley

Madam, your penance done, throw off this sheet and go we to attire you for our journey.

Duchess

My shame will not be shifted with my sheet, no, it will hang upon my richest robes snd show itself, attire me how I can.

Go, lead the way

I long to see my prison.

(Exit)

Act 3 Scene 1

The Abbey at Bury St. Edmund's.

(A sennet sounds)

(King Henry VI, Queen Margaret, Cardinal, Suffolk, York, Buckingham, Salisbury and Warwick enter to the Parliament)

King Henry VI

I muse my Lord of Gloucester is not come, it is not his wont to be the hindmost man, whatever occasion keeps him from us now.

Queen Margaret

Can you not see? or will ye not observe the strangeness of his altered countenance?

With what a majesty he bears himself, how insolent of late he is become, how proud, how peremptory, and unlike himself?

We know the time since he was mild and affable, and if we did but glance a far-off look, immediately he was upon his knee, that all the court admired him for submission

But meet him now, and, be it in the morn, when every one will give the time of day, he knits his brow and shows an angry eye, and passeth by with stiff unbowed knee, disdaining duty that to us belongs.

Small curs are not regarded when they grin

But great men tremble when the lion roars

And Humphrey is no little man in England.

First note that he is near you in descent, and should you fall, he as the next will mount.

Me seemeth then it is no policy respecting what a rancorous mind he bears, And his advantage following your decease, that he should come about your royal person or be admitted to your highness' council.

By flattery hath he won the commons' hearts, and when he please to make commotion, it is to be feared they all will follow him.

Now it is the spring, and weeds are shallow-rooted

Suffer them now, and they'll overgrow the garden and choke the herbs for want of husbandry.

The reverent care I bear unto my lord made me collect these dangers in the duke.

If it be fond, call it a woman's fear

Which fear if better reasons can supplant, I will subscribe and say I wronged the duke.

My Lord of Suffolk, Buckingham, and York, reprove my allegation, if you can or else conclude my words effectual.

Suffolk

Well hath your highness seen into this duke

And, had I first been put to speak my mind, I think I should have told your grace's tale.

The duchess, by his subornation, upon my life, began her devilish practises

Or, if he were not privy to those faults, yet, by reputing of his high descent, as next the king he was successive heir, and such high vaunts of his nobility, did instigate the bedlam brain-sick duchess by wicked means to frame our sovereign's fall.

Smooth runs the water where the brook is deep

And in his simple show he harbours treason.

The fox barks not when he would steal the lamb.

No, no, my sovereign

Gloucester is a man unsounded yet and full of deep deceit.

Cardinal

Did he not, contrary to form of law, devise strange deaths for small offences done?

York

And did he not, in his protectorship, Levy great sums of money through the realm for soldiers' pay in France, and never sent it?

By means whereof the towns each day revolted.

Buckingham

Tut, these are petty faults to faults unknown.

Which time will bring to light in smooth Duke Humphrey.

King Henry VI

My lords, at once, the care you have of us, to mow down thorns that would annoy our foot, is worthy praise, but shall I speak my conscience, our kinsman Gloucester is as innocent from meaning treason to our royal person

As is the sucking lamb or harmless dove, the duke is virtuous, mild and too well given to dream on evil or to work my downfall.

Queen Margaret

Ah, what's more dangerous than this fond affiance!

Seems he a dove? his feathers are but borrowed, for he's disposed as the hateful raven

Is he a lamb? his skin is surely lent him, for he's inclined as is the ravenous wolf.

Who cannot steal a shape that means deceit?

Take heed, my lord

The welfare of us all hangs on the cutting short that fraudful man.

(Somerset enters)

Somerset

All health unto my gracious sovereign!

King Henry VI

Welcome, Lord Somerset. What news from France?

Somerset

That all your interest in those territories is utterly bereft you

All is lost.

King Henry VI

Cold news, Lord Somerset, but God's will be done!

York

(From Aside) Cold news for me

For I had hope of France as firmly as I hope for fertile England.

Thus are my blossoms blasted in the bud and caterpillars eat my leaves away

But I will remedy this gear ere long, or sell my title for a glorious grave.

(Gloucester enters)

Gloucester

All happiness unto my lord the king!

Pardon, my liege, that I have stayed so long.

Suffolk

Nay, Gloucester, know that thou art come too soon, unless thou wert more loyal than thou art, I do arrest thee of high treason here.

Gloucester

Well, Suffolk, thou shalt not see me blush nor change my countenance for this arrest, a heart unspotted is not easily daunted.

The purest spring is not so free from mud as I am clear from treason to my sovereign, who can accuse me?

Wherein am I guilty?

York

It is thought, my lord, that you took bribes of France, and being protector stayed the soldiers' pay

By means whereof his highness hath lost France.

Gloucester

Is it but thought so? what are they that think it?

I never robbed the soldiers of their pay, nor ever had one penny bribe from France.

So help me God, as I have watched the night, ay, night by night, in studying good for England, that do it that ever I wrested from the king, or any groat I hoarded to my use, be brought against me at my trial-day!

No

Many a pound of mine own proper store, because I would not tax the needy commons, have I disbursed to the garrisons, and never asked for restitution.

Cardinal

It serves you well, my lord, to say so much.

Gloucester

I say no more than truth, so help me God!

York

In your protectorship you did devise strange tortures for offenders never heard of, that England was defamed by tyranny.

Gloucester

Why, it is well known that, whiles I was protector,

Pity was all the fault that was in me

For I should melt at an offender's tears, and lowly words were ransom for their fault.

Unless it were a bloody murderer, or foul felonious thief that fleeced poor passengers, I never gave them condign punishment

Murder indeed, that bloody sin, I tortured above the felon or what trespass else.

Suffolk

My lord, these faults are easy, quickly answered, but mightier crimes are laid unto your charge whereof you cannot easily purge yourself.

I do arrest you in his highness' name

And here commit you to my lord cardinal yo keep, until your further time of trial.

King Henry VI

My lord of Gloucester, it is my special hope that you will clear yourself from all suspect, my conscience tells me you are innocent.

Gloucester

Ah, gracious lord, these days are dangerous, virtue is choked with foul ambition and charity chased hence by rancour's hand

Foul subornation is predominant and equity exiled your highness' land.

I know their complot is to have my life, and if my death might make this island happy, and prove the period of their tyranny, I would expend it with all willingness, but mine is made the prologue to their play

For thousands more, that yet suspect no peril, will not conclude their plotted tragedy.

Beaufort's red sparkling eyes blab his heart's malice, and Suffolk's cloudy brow his stormy hate

Sharp Buckingham unburthens with his tongue the envious load that lies upon his heart

And dogged York, that reaches at the moon, whose overweening arm I have plucked back, by false accuse doth level at my life

And you, my sovereign lady, with the rest, causeless have laid disgraces on my head, and with your best endeavour have stirred up my liefest liege to be mine enemy

Ay, all you have laid your heads together...

Myself had notice of your conventicles...

And all to make away my guiltless life.

I shall not want false witness to condemn me, nor store of treasons to augment my guilt

The ancient proverb will be well effected, a staff is quickly found to beat a dog.

Cardinal

My liege, his railing is intolerable, if those that care to keep your royal person from treason's secret knife and traitors' rage be thus upbraided, chid and rated at, and the offender granted scope of speech

It will make them cool in zeal unto your grace.

Suffolk

Hath he not twit our sovereign lady here with ignominious words, though clerkly couched, as if she had suborned some to swear false allegations to overthrow his state?

Queen Margaret

But I can give the loser leave to chide.

Gloucester

Far truer spoke than meant: I lose, indeed

Beshrew the winners, for they played me false! And well such losers may have leave to speak.

Buckingham

He'll wrest the sense and hold us here all day, Lord cardinal, he is your prisoner.

Cardinal

Sirs, take away the duke, and guard him sure.

Gloucester

Ah! thus King Henry throws away his crutch before his legs be firm to bear his body.

Thus is the shepherd beaten from thy side, and wolves are gnarling who shall gnaw thee first.

Ah, that my fear were false! ah, that it were!

For, good King Henry, thy decay I fear.

(exits guarded)

King Henry VI

My lords, what to your wisdoms seemeth best, do or undo, as if ourself were here.

Queen Margaret

What, will your highness leave the parliament?

King Henry VI

Ay, Margaret; my heart is drown'd with grief, whose flood begins to flow within mine eyes, my body round engirt with misery, for what's more miserable than discontent?

Ah, uncle Humphrey! in thy face I see the map of honour, truth and loyalty, and yet good Humphrey is the hour to come that ever I proved thee false or feared thy faith.

What louring star now envies thy estate, that these great lords and Margaret our queen do seek subversion of thy harmless life?

Thou never didst them wrong, nor no man wrong

And as the butcher takes away the calf and binds the wretch, and beats it when it strays, bearing it to the bloody slaughter-house, even so remorseless have they borne him hence

And as the dam runs lowing up and down, looking the way her harmless young one went, and can do nought but wail her darling's loss

Even so myself bewails good Gloucester's case with sad unhelpful tears, and with dimmed eyes look after him and cannot do him good, do mighty are his vowed enemies.

His fortunes I will weep

And between each groan say who's a traitor? Gloucester he is none.

(All but Queen Margaret, Cardinal, Suffolk, and York exit, Somerset remains apart)

Queen Margaret

Free lords, cold snow melts with the sun's hot beams.

Henry my lord is cold in great affairs, too full of foolish pity, and Gloucester's show beguiles him as the mournful crocodile with sorrow snares relenting passengers, or as the snake rolled in a flowering bank with shining chequered slough, doth sting a child that for the beauty thinks it excellent.

Believe me, lords, were none more wise than I…

And yet herein I judge mine own wit good…

This Gloucester should be quickly rid the world, to rid us of the fear we have of him.

Cardinal

That he should die is worthy policy

But yet we want a colour for his death, it is met he be condemned by course of law.

Suffolk

But, in my mind, that were no policy, the king will labour still to save his life, the commons haply rise, to save his life

And yet we have but trivial argument, more than mistrust, that shows him worthy death.

York

So that, by this, you would not have him die.

Suffolk

Ah, York, no man alive so fain as I!

York

It is York that hath more reason for his death.

But, my lord cardinal, and you my Lord of Suffolk, say as you think, and speak it from your souls

Were it not all one, an empty eagle were set to guard the chicken from a hungry kite, as place Duke Humphrey for the king's protector?

Queen Margaret

So the poor chicken should be sure of death.

Suffolk

Madam, 'tis true; and were it not madness, then to make the fox surveyor of the fold?

Who being accused a crafty murderer, his guilt should be but idly posted over because his purpose is not executed.

No

Let him die, in that he is a fox by nature proved an enemy to the flock, before his chaps be stained with crimson blood as Humphrey, proved by reasons to my liege.

And do not stand on quillets how to slay him

Be it by gins, by snares, by subtlety sleeping or waking, it is no matter how, so he be dead

For that is good deceit which mates him first that first intends deceit.

Queen Margaret

Thrice-noble Suffolk, it is resolutely spoke.

Suffolk

Not resolute, except so much were done

For things are often spoke and seldom meant, but that my heart accordeth with my tongue, seeing the deed is meritorious and to preserve my sovereign from his foe

Say but the word, and I will be his priest.

Cardinal

But I would have him dead, my Lord of Suffolk, here you can take due orders for a priest

Say you consent and censure well the deed and I'll provide his executioner, I tender so the safety of my liege.

Suffolk

Here is my hand, the deed is worthy doing.

Queen Margaret

And so say I.

York

And I and now we three have spoke it, it skills not greatly who impugns our doom.

(A Post enters)

Post

Great lords, from Ireland am I come a main, to signify that rebels there are up and put the Englishmen unto the sword

Send succors, lords, and stop the rage bedtime, before the wound do grow uncurable

For, being green there is great hope of help.

Cardinal

A breach that craves a quick expedient stop!

What counsel give you in this weighty cause?

York

That Somerset be sent as regent thither

It is meet that lucky ruler be employ'd

Witness the fortune he hath had in France.

Somerset

If York, with all his far-fet policy, had been the regent there instead of me, he never would have stayed in France so long.

York

No, not to lose it all, as thou hast done

I rather would have lost my life betimes than bring a burthen of dishonour home by staying there so long till all were lost.

Show me one scar charactered on thy skin

Men's flesh preserved so whole do seldom win.

Queen Margaret

Nay then, this spark will prove a raging fire, if wind and fuel be brought to feed it with

No more good York

Sweet Somerset be still

Thy fortune, York, hadst thou been regent there, might happily have proved far worse than his.

York

What, worse than nought?

Nay, then a shame take all!

Somerset

And, in the number, thee that wishest shame!

Cardinal

My Lord of York, try what your fortune is.

The uncivil kerns of Ireland are in arms and temper clay with blood of Englishmen

To Ireland will you lead a band of men, collected choicely from each county some, and try your hap against the Irishmen?

York

I will, my lord, so please his majesty.

Suffolk

Why, our authority is his consent, and what we do establish he confirms

Then, noble York, take thou this task in hand.

York

I am content: provide me soldiers, lords, whiles I take order for mine own affairs.

Suffolk

A charge, Lord York, that I will see performed.

But now return we to the false Duke Humphrey.

Cardinal

No more of him; for I will deal with him that henceforth he shall trouble us no more.

And so break off

The day is almost spent, Lord Suffolk, you and I must talk of that event.

York

My Lord of Suffolk, within fourteen days at Bristol I expect my soldiers

For there I'll ship them all for Ireland.

Suffolk

I'll see it truly done, my Lord of York.

(All but York exit)

York

Now, York, or never, steel thy fearful thoughts, and change misdoubt to resolution

Be that thou hopest to be, or what thou art resign to death; it is not worth the enjoying

Let pale-faced fear keep with the mean-born man, and find no harbour in a royal heart.

Faster than spring-time showers comes thought on thought, and not a thought but thinks on dignity.

My brain more busy than the labouring spider weaves tedious snares to trap mine enemies.

Well, nobles, well, it is politicly done, to send me packing with an host of men

I fear me you but warm the starved snake, who cherished in your breasts will sting your hearts.

It was men I lacked and you will give them me

I take it kindly

Yet be well assured you put sharp weapons in a madman's hands.

Whiles I in Ireland nourish a mighty band, I will stir up in England some black storm shall blow ten thousand souls to heaven or hell

This fell tempest shall not cease to rage until the golden circuit on my head, like to the glorious sun's transparent beams do calm the fury of this mad-bred flaw.

And, for a minister of my intent, I have seduced a headstrong Kentishman, John Cade of Ashford, to make commotion, as full well he can under the title of John Mortimer.

In Ireland have I seen this stubborn Cade Oppose himself against a troop of kerns, and fought so long, till that his thighs with darts were almost like a sharp-quilled porpentine

And, in the end being rescued, I have seen him caper upright like a wild Morisco, shaking the bloody darts as he his bells.

Full often, like a shag-haired crafty kern, hath he conversed with the enemy, and undiscovered come to me again and given me notice of their villanies.

This devil here shall be my substitute for that John Mortimer, which now is dead, in face, in gait, in speech, he doth resemble

By this I shall perceive the commons' mind how they affect the house and claim of York.

Say he be taken, racked and tortured, I know no pain they can inflict upon him will make him say I moved him to those arms.

Say that he thrive, as it is great like he will, why then from Ireland come I with my strength and reap the harvest which that rascal sowed, for Humphrey being dead, as he shall be, and Henry put apart the next for me.

(Exit)

Act 3 Scene 2

Bury St. Edmund's. A room of state.

(Certain Murderers enter, hastily)

First Murderer

Run to my Lord of Suffolk

Let him know we have dispatched the duke, as he commanded.

Second Murderer

Oh that it were to do! What have we done?

Didst ever hear a man so penitent?

(Suffolk enters)

First Murder

Here comes my lord.

Suffolk

Now, sirs, have you dispatched this thing?

First Murderer

Ay, my good lord, he's dead.

Suffolk

Why, that's well said.

Go, get you to my house

I will reward you for this venturous deed.

The king and all the peers are here at hand.

Have you laid fair the bed? Is all things well, according as I gave directions?

First Murderer

It is, my good lord.

Suffolk

Away! be gone.

(Murderers exit)

(Trumpets sound)

(King Henry VI, Queen Margaret, Cardinal, Somerset, with Attendants enter)

King Henry VI

Go, call our uncle to our presence straight

Say we intend to try his grace to-day.

If he be guilty, as it is published.

Suffolk

I'll call him presently, my noble lord.

(Exit)

King Henry VI

Lords, take your places; and, I pray you all, proceed no straighter against our uncle Gloucester than from true evidence of good esteem he be approved in practice culpable.

Queen Margaret

God forbid any malice should prevail that faultless may condemn a nobleman!

Pray God he may acquit him of suspicion!

King Henry VI

I thank thee, Meg; these words content me much.

(Suffolk re-enters)

How now! why look'st thou pale? why tremblest thou?

Where is our uncle? what's the matter, Suffolk?

Suffolk

Dead in his bed, my lord

Gloucester is dead.

Queen Margaret

Marry, God forfend!

Cardinal

God's secret judgment, I did dream to-night the duke was dumb and could not speak a word.

(King Henry VI swoons)

Queen Margaret

How fares my lord? Help, lords! the king is dead.

Somerset

Rear up his body

Wring him by the nose.

Queen Margaret

Run, go, help, help! Oh Henry, open thine eyes!

Suffolk

He doth revive again: madam, be patient.

King Henry VI

Oh heavenly God!

Queen Margaret

How fares my gracious lord?

Suffolk

Comfort, my sovereign! Gracious Henry, comfort!

King Henry VI

What, doth my Lord of Suffolk comfort me?

Came he right now to sing a raven's note whose dismal tune bereft my vital powers

Thinks he that the chirping of a wrench by crying comfort from a hollow breast can chase away the first-conceived sound?

Hide not thy poison with such sugared words

Lay not thy hands on me

Forbear, I say

Their touch affrights me as a serpent's sting.

Thou baleful messenger, out of my sight!

Upon thy eye-balls murderous tyranny sits in grim majesty, to fright the world.

Look not upon me, for thine eyes are wounding, yet do not go away

Come, basilisk, and kill the innocent gazer with thy sight

For in the shade of death I shall find joy in life but double death, now Gloucester's dead.

Queen Margaret

Why do you rate my Lord of Suffolk thus?

Although the duke was enemy to him, yet he most Christian-like laments his death, and for myself, foe as he was to me, might liquid tears or heart-offending groans or blood-consuming sighs recall his life

I would be blind with weeping, sick with groans, look pale as primrose with blood-drinking sighs, and all to have the noble duke alive.

What know I how the world may deem of me?

For it is known we were but hollow friends, it may be judged I made the duke away

So shall my name with slander's tongue be wounded, and princes' courts be filled with my reproach.

This get I by his death, ay me, unhappy!

To be a queen, and crowned with infamy!

King Henry VI

Ah, woe is me for Gloucester, wretched man!

Queen Margaret

Be woe for me, more wretched than he is.

What, dost thou turn away and hide thy face?

I am no loathsome leper

Look on me.

What! art thou, like the adder, waxen deaf?

Be poisonous too and kill thy forlorn queen.

Is all thy comfort shut in Gloucester's tomb?

Why, then, dame Margaret was never thy joy.

Erect his statue and worship it, and make my image but an alehouse sign.

Was I for this nigh wrecked upon the sea and twice by awkward wind from England's bank drove back again unto my native clime?

What boded this, but well forewarning wind did seem to say seek not a scorpion's nest, nor set no footing on this unkind shore?

What did I then, but cursed the gentle gusts and he that loosed them forth their brazen caves, and bid them blow towards England's blessed shore, or turn our stern upon a dreadful rock

Yet Aeolus would not be a murderer, but left that hateful office unto thee

The pretty-vaulting sea refused to drown me knowing that thou wouldst have me drowned on shore With tears as salt as sea, through thy unkindness

The splitting rocks cowered in the sinking sands and would not dash me with their ragged sides because thy flinty heart, more hard than they might in thy palace perish Margaret.

As far as I could ken thy chalky cliffs, when from thy shore the tempest beat us back, I stood upon the hatches in the storm, and when the dusky sky began to rob my earnest-gaping sight of thy land's view, I took a costly jewel from my neck.

A heart it was, bound in with diamonds, and threw it towards thy land

The sea received it, and so I wished thy body might my heart, and even with this I lost fair England's view, and bid mine eyes be packing with my heart, and called them blind and dusky spectacles for losing ken of Albion's wished coast.

How often have I tempted Suffolk's tongue, the agent of thy foul inconstancy, to sit and witch me, as Ascanius did when he to madding Dido would unfold his father's acts commenced in burning Troy!

Am I not witched like her? or thou not false like him?

Ay me, I can no more! die, Margaret!

For Henry weeps that thou dost live so long.

(Noise within)

(Warwick, Salisbury, and many Commons enter)

Warwick

It is reported, mighty sovereign, that good Duke Humphrey traitorously is murdered by Suffolk and the Cardinal Beaufort's means.

The commons, like an angry hive of bees that want their leader, scatter up and down and care not who they sting in his revenge.

Myself have calmed their spleenful mutiny, until they hear the order of his death.

King Henry VI

That he is dead, good Warwick, 'tis too true

How he died God knows, not Henry

Enter his chamber, view his breathless corpse and comment then upon his sudden death.

Warwick

That shall I do, my liege.

Stay, Salisbury, with the rude multitude till I return.

(Exit)

King Henry VI

Oh thou that judgest all things, stay my thoughts, my thoughts, that labour to persuade my soul some violent hands were laid on Humphrey's life!

If my suspect be false, forgive me, God, for judgment only doth belong to thee.

Fain would I go to chafe his paly lips with twenty thousand kisses, and to drain upon his face an ocean of salt tears, to tell my love unto his dumb deaf trunk, and with my fingers feel his hand unfeeling

But all in vain are these mean obsequies

And to survey his dead and earthly image, what were it but to make my sorrow greater?

(Warwick and others enter, bearing Gloucester's body on a bed)

Warwick

Come hither, gracious sovereign, view this body.

King Henry VI

That is to see how deep my grave is made

For with his soul fled all my worldly solace, for seeing him I see my life in death.

Warwick

As surely as my soul intends to live with that dread King that took our state upon him to free us from his father's wrathful curse,

I do believe that violent hands were laid upon the life of this thrice-famed duke.

Suffolk

A dreadful oath, sworn with a solemn tongue!

What instance gives Lord Warwick for his vow?

Warwick

See how the blood is settled in his face.

Oft have I seen a timely-parted ghost, of ashy semblance, meagre, pale and bloodless, being all descended to the labouring heart

Who, in the conflict that it holds with death attracts the same for audience against the enemy

Which with the heart there cools and never returneth to blush and beautify the cheek again.

But see, his face is black and full of blood, his eye-balls further out than when he lived, staring full ghastly like a strangled man

His hair upreared, his nostrils stretched with struggling

His hands abroad displayed, as one that grasped and tugged for life and was by strength subdued

Look, on the sheets his hair you see, is sticking

His well-proportioned beard made rough and rugged like to the summer's corn by tempest lodged.

It cannot be but he was murdered here

The least of all these signs were probable.

Suffolk

Why, Warwick, who should do the duke to death?

Myself and Beaufort had him in protection

We, I hope, sir, are no murderers.

Warwick

But both of you were vowed Duke Humphrey's foes, and you, forsooth, had the good duke to keep

It is like you would not feast him like a friend

It is well seen he found an enemy.

Queen Margaret

Then you, belike, suspect these noblemen as guilty of Duke Humphrey's timeless death.

Warwick

Who finds the heifer dead and bleeding fresh and sees fast by a butcher with an axe, but will suspect it was he that made the slaughter?

Who finds the partridge in the buttock's nest, but may imagine how the bird was dead, although the kite soar with unbloodied beak?

Even so suspicious is this tragedy.

Queen Margaret

Are you the butcher, Suffolk? Where's your knife?

Is Beaufort termed a kite? Where are his talons?

Suffolk

I wear no knife to slaughter sleeping men

Here's a vengeful sword, rusted with ease, that shall be scoured in his rancorous heart that slanders me with murder's crimson badge.

Say, if thou darest, proud Lord of Warwick-shire, that I am faulty in Duke Humphrey's death.

(Cardinal, Somerset, and others exit)

Warwick

What dares not Warwick, if false Suffolk dare him?

Queen Margaret

He dares not calm his contumelious spirit nor cease to be an arrogant controller, though Suffolk dare him twenty thousand times.

Warwick

Madam, be still; with reverence may I say

For every word you speak in his behalf is slander to your royal dignity.

Suffolk

Blunt-witted lord, ignoble in demeanor!

If ever lady wronged her lord so much, thy mother took into her blameful bed, some stern untutored churl, and noble stock was graft with crab-tree slip

Whose fruit thou art, and never of the Nevils' noble race.

Warwick

But that the guilt of murder bucklers thee and I should rob the deathsman of his fee, quitting thee thereby of ten thousand shames, and that my sovereign's presence makes me mild, I would, false murderous coward, on thy knee make thee beg pardon for thy passed speech,

And say it was thy mother that thou meant'st that thou thyself was born in bastardy

After all this fearful homage done give thee thy hire and send thy soul to hell, pernicious blood-sucker of sleeping men!

Suffolk

Thou shall be waking well I shed thy blood, if from this presence thou darest go with me.

Warwick

Away even now, or I will drag thee hence

Unworthy though thou art, I'll cope with thee and do some service to Duke Humphrey's ghost.

(Suffolk and Warwick exit)

King Henry VI

What stronger breastplate than a heart untainted!

Thrice is he armed that hath his quarrel just, and he but naked though locked up in steel, Wwhose conscience with injustice is corrupted.

(A noise within)

Queen Margaret

What noise is this?

(Suffolk and Warwick re-enter, with their weapons drawn)

King Henry VI

Why, how now, lords! your wrathful weapons drawn here in our presence! dare you be so bold?

Why, what tumultuous clamour have we here?

Suffolk

The traitorous Warwick with the men of Bury set all upon me, mighty sovereign.

Salisbury

(To the Commons, entering) Sirs, stand apart

The king shall know your mind.

Dread lord, the commons send you word by me, unless Lord Suffolk straight be done to death or banished fair England's territories,

They will by violence tear him from your palace and torture him with grievous lingering death.

They say, by him the good Duke Humphrey died

They say, in him they fear your highness' death

Mere instinct of love and loyalty, free from a stubborn opposite intent, as being thought to contradict your liking, makes them thus forward in his banishment.

They say, in care of your most royal person, that if your highness should intend to sleep and charge that no man should disturb your rest in pain of your dislike or pain of death

Yet, notwithstanding such a strait edict were there a serpent seen, with forked tongue, that slily glided towards your majesty

It were but necessary you were waked, lest being suffered in that harmful slumber, the mortal worm might make the sleep eternal

Therefore do they cry, though you forbid, that they will guard you, whether you will or no, from such fell serpents as false Suffolk is with whose envenomed and fatal sting your loving uncle

Twenty times his worth they say, is shamefully bereft of life.

Commons

(Within) An answer from the king, my Lord of Salisbury!

Suffolk

It is like the commons, rude unpolished hinds, could send such message to their sovereign

You, my lord, were glad to be employed, to show how quaint an orator you are

All the honour Salisbury hath won is that he was the lord ambassador sent from a sort of tinkers to the king.

Commons

(Within) An answer from the king, or we will all break in!

King Henry VI

Go, Salisbury, and tell them all from me.

I thank them for their tender loving care

Had I not been cited so by them, yet did I purpose as they do entreat

For, sure, my thoughts do hourly prophesy mischance unto my state by Suffolk's means, and therefore by His majesty I swear, whose far unworthy deputy I am

He shall not breathe infection in this air but three days longer, on the pain of death.

(Salisbury exits)

Queen Margaret

Oh Henry, let me plead for gentle Suffolk!

King Henry VI

Ungentle queen, to call him gentle Suffolk!

No more, I say, if thou dost plead for him, thou wilt but add increase unto my wrath.

Had I but said, I would have kept my word, but when I swear, it is irrevocable.

If, after three days' space, thou here best found on any ground that I am ruler of, the world shall not be ransom for thy life.

Come, Warwick, come, good Warwick, go with me

I have great matters to impart to thee.

(All but Queen Margaret and Suffolk exit)

Queen Margaret

Mischance and sorrow go along with you!

Heart's discontent and sour affliction

Be playfellows to keep you company!

There's two of you; the devil make a third!

And threefold vengeance tend upon your steps!

Suffolk

Cease these execrations gentle queen, and let thy Suffolk take his heavy leave.

Queen Margaret

Fie, coward woman and soft-hearted wretch!

Hast thou not spirit to curse thine enemy?

Suffolk

A plague upon them! wherefore should I curse them?

Would curses kill, as doth the mandrake's groan, I would invent as bitter-searching terms, as curst, as harsh and horrible to hear delivered strongly through my fixed teeth,

With full as many signs of deadly hate, as lean-faced Envy in her loathsome cave

My tongue should stumble in mine earnest words

Mine eyes should sparkle like the beaten flint

Mine hair be fixed on end, as one distract

Ay, every joint should seem to curse and ban, and even now my burthened heart would break, should I not curse them.

Poison be their drink!

Gall, worse than gall, the daintiest that they taste!

Their sweetest shade a grove of cypress trees!

Their chiefest prospect murdering basilisks!

Their softest touch as smart as lizards' sting!

Their music frightful as the serpent's hiss, and boding screech-owls make the concert full!

All the foul terrors in dark-seated hell…

Queen Margaret

Enough, sweet Suffolk; thou torment'st thyself

These dread curses, like the sun against glass, or like an overcharged gun, recoil and turn the force of them upon thyself.

Suffolk

You bade me ban, and will you bid me leave?

Now, by the ground that I am banished from, well could I curse away a winter's night, though standing naked on a mountain top where biting cold would never let grass grow and think it but a minute spent in sport.

Queen Margaret

Oh, let me entreat thee cease.

Give me thy hand, that I may dew it with my mournful tears

Nor let the rain of heaven wet this place to wash away my woeful monuments.

Oh, could this kiss be printed in thy hand, that thou mightst think upon these by the seal, through whom a thousand sighs are breathed for thee!

So, get thee gone, that I may know my grief

It is but surmised whiles thou art standing by as one that surfeits thinking on a want.

I will repeal thee, or, be well assured, adventure to be banished myself, and banished I am, if but from thee.

Go

Speak not to me; even now be gone.

Oh, go not yet! Even thus two friends condemned embrace and kiss and take ten thousand leaves, loather a hundred times to part than die.

Yet now farewell; and farewell life with thee!

Suffolk

Thus is poor Suffolk ten times banished

Once by the king, and three times thrice by thee.

It is not the land I care for, wert thou thence

A wilderness is populous enough, so Suffolk had thy heavenly company, for where thou art, there is the world itself with every several pleasure in the world, and where thou art not desolation.

I can no more, live thou to joy thy life

Myself no joy in nought but that thou livest.

(Vaux enters)

Queen Margaret

Wither goes Vaux so fast? what news, I pray to thee?

Vaux

To signify unto his majesty that Cardinal Beaufort is at point of death

For suddenly a grievous sickness took him that makes him gasp and stare and catch the air, blaspheming God and cursing men on earth.

Sometimes he talks as if Duke Humphrey's ghost were by his side

Sometime he calls the king snd whispers to his pillow, as to him the secrets of his overcharged soul

I am sent to tell his majesty that even now he cries aloud for him.

Queen Margaret

Go tell this heavy message to the king.

(Vaux exits)

Ay me! what is this world! what news are these!

But wherefore grieve I at an hour's poor loss, omitting Suffolk's exile, my soul's treasure?

Why only, Suffolk, mourn I not for thee and with the southern clouds contend in tears, theirs for the earth's increase, mine for my sorrows?

Now get thee hence: the king, thou know'st, is coming

If thou be found by me, thou art but dead.

Suffolk

If I depart from thee, I cannot live

In thy sight to die, what were it else but like a pleasant slumber in thy lap?

Here could I breathe my soul into the air, as mild and gentle as the cradle-babe dying with mother's dug between its lips

Where, from thy sight, I should be raging mad, and cry out for thee to close up mine eyes to have thee with thy lips to stop my mouth

So shouldst thou either turn my flying soul, or I should breathe it so into thy body, and then it lived in sweet Elysium.

To die by thee were but to die in jest

From thee to die were torture more than death

Oh, let me stay, befall what may befall!

Queen Margaret

Away! though parting be a fretful corrosive, it is applied to a deathful wound.

To France, sweet Suffolk, let me hear from thee

For wheresoever thou art in this world's globe, I'll have an Iris that shall find thee out.

Suffolk

I go.

Queen Margaret

And take my heart with thee.

Suffolk

A jewel, locked into the wofull'st cask that ever did contain a thing of worth.

Even as a splitted bark, so sunder we this way fall I to death.

Queen Margaret

This way for me.

(severally exit)

Act 3 Scene 3

A bedchamber.

(The King, Salisbury, Warwick enter, meeting the Cardinal in bed)

King Henry VI

How fares my lord? speak, Beaufort, to thy sovereign.

Cardinal

If thou be'st death, I'll give thee England's treasure, enough to purchase such another island, so thou wilt let me live, and feel no pain.

King Henry VI

Ah, what a sign it is of evil life, where death's approach is seen so terrible!

Warwick

Beaufort, it is thy sovereign speaks to thee.

Cardinal

Bring me unto my trial when you will.

Died he not in his bed? where should he die?

Can I make men live, whether they will or no?

Oh, torture me no more! I will confess.

Alive again? then show me where he is, I'll give a thousand pound to look upon him.

He hath no eyes, the dust hath blinded them.

Comb down his hair; look, look! it stands upright like lime-twigs set to catch my winged soul.

Give me some drink

Bid the apothecary bring the strong poison that I bought of him.

King Henry VI

Oh thou eternal Mover of the heavens.

Look with a gentle eye upon this wretch!

Oh, beat away the busy meddling fiend that lays strong siege unto this wretch's soul.

And from his bosom purge this black despair!

Warwick

See, how the pangs of death do make him grin!

Salisbury

Disturb him not

Let him pass peaceably.

King Henry VI

Peace to his soul, if God's good pleasure be!

Lord cardinal, if thou think'st on heaven's bliss, hold up thy hand, make signal of thy hope.

He dies, and makes no sign. Oh God, forgive him!

Warwick

So bad a death argues a monstrous life.

King Henry VI

Forbear to judge, for we are sinners all.

Close up his eyes and draw the curtain close

Let us all to meditation.

(Exit)

Act 4 Scene 1

The coast of Kent.

(Alarum)

A fight at sea, ordnance goes off.

(A Captain, a Master, a Master's-mate, Walter Whitmore, and others enter, with them Suffolk, and others, prisoners)

Captain

The gaudy, blabbing and remorseful day is crept into the bosom of the sea

Now loud-howling wolves arouse the jades that drag the tragic melancholy night

Who, with their drowsy, slow and flagging wings, clip dead men's graves and from their misty jaws breathe foul contagious darkness in the air.

Therefore bring forth the soldiers of our prize

For, whilst our pinnace anchors in the Downs, here shall they make their ransom on the sand, or with their blood stain this discoloured shore.

Master, this prisoner freely give I thee

Thou that art his mate, make boot of this

The other, Walter Whitmore, is thy share.

First Gentleman

What is my ransom, master? let me know.

Master

A thousand crowns, or else lay down your head.

Master's-Mate,and so much shall you give, or off goes yours.

Captain

What, think you much to pay two thousand crowns, and bear the name and port of gentlemen?

Cut both the villains' throats; for die you shall, the lives of those which we have lost in fight be counterpoised with such a petty sum!

First Gentleman

I'll give it, sir; and therefore spare my life.

Second Gentleman

And so will I and write home for it straight.

Whitmore

I lost mine eye in laying the prize aboard, and therefore to revenge it, shalt thou die

(To Suffolk

And so should these, if I might have my will.

Captain

Be not so rash; take ransom, let him live.

Suffolk

Look on my George; I am a gentleman, rate me at what thou wilt, thou shalt be paid.

Whitmore

And so am I

My name is Walter Whitmore.

How now! why start'st thou?

What, doth death affright?

Suffolk

Thy name affrights me, in whose sound is death.

A cunning man did calculate my birth and told me that by water I should die, yet let not this make thee be bloody-minded

Thy name is Gaultier, being rightly sounded.

Whitmore

Gaultier or Walter, which it is, I care not, never yet did base dishonour blur our name, but with our sword we wiped away the blot

When merchant-like I sell revenge, broke be my sword, my arms torn and defaced, and I proclaimed a coward through the world!

Suffolk

Stay, Whitmore; for thy prisoner is a prince, the Duke of Suffolk, William de la Pole.

Whitmore

The Duke of Suffolk muffled up in rags!

Suffolk

Ay, but these rags are no part of the duke, Jupiter sometimes went disguised, and why not I?

Captain

But Jove was never slain, as thou shalt be.

Suffolk

Obscure and lowly swain, King Henry's blood, the honourable blood of Lancaster, must not be shed by such a jaded groom.

Hast thou not kissed thy hand and held my stirrup?

Bare-headed plodded by my foot-cloth mule and thought thee happy when I shook my head?

How often hast thou waited at my cup, fed from my trencher, kneeled down at the board.

When I have feasted with Queen Margaret?

Remember it and let it make thee crest-fallen, ay, and allay this thy abortive pride

How in our voiding lobby hast thou stood and duly waited for my coming forth?

This hand of mine hath writ in thy behalf, and therefore shall it charm thy riotous tongue.

Whitmore

Speak, captain, shall I stab the forlorn swain?

Captain

First let my words stab him, as he hath me.

Suffolk

Base slave, thy words are blunt and so art thou.

Captain

Convey him hence and on our longboat's side strike off his head.

Suffolk

Thou darest not, for thy own.

Captain

Yes, Pole.

Suffolk

Pole!

Captain

Pool! Sir Pool! lord!

Ay, kennel, puddle, sink

Whose filth and dirt troubles the silver spring where England drinks.

Now will I dam up this thy yawning mouth for swallowing the treasure of the realm, thy lips that kissed the queen shall sweep the ground

Thou that smiledst at good Duke Humphrey's death, against the senseless winds shalt grin in vain, who in contempt shall hiss at thee again, and wedded be thou to the hags of hell.

For daring to off a mighty lord unto the daughter of a worthless king, having neither subject, wealth, nor diadem. by devilish policy art thou grown great, and, like ambitious Sylla, overgorged with gobbets of thy mother's bleeding heart.

By thee Anjou and Maine were sold to France, the false revolting Normans thorough thee disdain to call us lord, and Picardy hath slain their governors, surprised our forts, and sent the ragged soldiers wounded home.

The princely Warwick, and the Nevils all, whose dreadful swords were never drawn in vain, as hating thee, are rising up in arms

And now the house of York, thrust from the crown by shameful murder of a guiltless king and lofty proud encroaching tyranny, burns with revenging fire

Whose hopeful colours advance our half-faced sun, striving to shine, under the which is writ 'Invitis nubibus.'

The commons here in Kent are up in arms

To conclude, reproach and beggary is crept into the palace of our king.

And all by thee. Away! convey him hence.

Suffolk

Oh that I were a god, to shoot forth thunder upon these paltry, servile, abject drudges!

Small things make base men proud, this villain here being captain of a pinnace, threatens more than Bargulus the strong Illyrian pirate.

Drones suck not eagles' blood but rob beehives, it is impossible that I should die by such a lowly vassal as thyself.

Thy words move rage and not remorse in me, I go of message from the queen to France

I charge thee waft me safely cross the Channel.

Captain

Walter…

Whitmore

Come, Suffolk, I must waft thee to thy death.

Suffolk

Gelidus timor occupat artus it is thee I fear.

Whitmore

Thou shalt have cause to fear before I leave thee.

What, are ye daunted now? now will ye stoop?

First Gentleman

My gracious lord, entreat him, speak him fair.

Suffolk

Suffolk's imperial tongue is stern and rough, used to command, untaught to plead for favour.

Far be it we should honour such as these with humble suit: no, rather let my head stoop to the block than these knees bow to any save to the God of heaven and to my king

Sooner dance upon a bloody pole than stand uncovered to the vulgar groom.

True nobility is exempt from fear, more can I bear than you dare execute.

Captain

Hale him away, and let him talk no more.

Suffolk

Come, soldiers, show what cruelty ye can, that this my death may never be forgot!

Great men oft die by vile bezonians, a Roman sworder and banditto slave murdered sweet Tully; Brutus' bastard hand stabbed Julius Caesar

Savage islanders Pompey the Great

Suffolk dies by pirates.

(Whitmore and others exit with Suffolk)

Captain

And as for these whose ransom we have set, it is our pleasure one of them depart

Therefore come you with us and let him go.

(All but the First Gentleman exit)

(Whitmore with Suffolk's body re-enter)

Whitmore

There let his head and lifeless body lie, until the queen his mistress bury it.

(Exit)

First Gentleman

Oh barbarous and bloody spectacle!

His body will I bear unto the king, if he revenge it not, yet will his friends

So will the queen, that living held him dear.

(Exits with the body)

Act 4 Scene 2

Blackheath.

(George Bevis and John Holland Bevis enter)

Come, and get thee a sword, though made of a lath

They have been up these two days.

Holland

They have the more need to sleep now, then.

Bevis

I tell thee, Jack Cade the clothier means to dress the commonwealth, and turn it, and set a new nap upon it.

Holland

So he had need, for it is threadbare.

Well, I say it was never merry world in England since gentlemen came up.

Bevis

Oh miserable age! Virtue is not regarded in handicrafts-men.

Holland

The nobility think scorn to go in leather aprons.

Bevis

Nay, more, the king's council are no good workmen.

Holland

True; and yet it is said, labour in thy vocation

Which is as much to say as, let the magistrates be labouring men

Therefore should we be magistrates.

Bevis

Thou hast hit it

There's no better sign of a brave mind than a hard hand.

Holland

I see them! I see them! there's Best's son, the tanner of Wingham…

Bevis

He shall have the skin of our enemies, to make dog's-leather of.

Holland

And Dick the Butcher…

Bevis

Then is sin struck down like an ox, and iniquity's throat cut like a calf.

Holland

And Smith the weaver…

Bevis

Argo, their thread of life is spun.

Holland

Come, come, let's fall in with them.

(Drum)

(Cade, Dick the Butcher, Smith the Weaver, and a Sawyer enter, with infinite numbers)

Cade

We John Cade, so termed of our supposed father…

Dick

(From Aside) Or rather, of stealing a cade of herrings.

Cade

For our enemies shall fall before us, inspired with the spirit of putting down kings and princes…

Command silence.

Dick

Silence!

Cade

My father was a Mortimer…

Dick

(From Aside) He was an honest man, and a good bricklayer.

Cade

My mother a Plantagenet…

Dick

(From Aside) I knew her well; she was a midwife.

Cade

My wife descended of the Lacies...

Dick

(From Aside) She was, indeed, a pedler's daughter, and sold many laces.

Smith

(From Aside) But now of late, notable to travel with her furred pack, she washes bucks here at home.

Cade

Therefore am I of an honourable house.

Dick

(From Aside) Ay, by my faith, the field is honourable

There was he borne, under a hedge, for his father had never a house but the cage.

Cade

Valiant I am.

Smith

(From Aside) A' must needs

For beggary is valiant.

Cade

I am able to endure much.

Dick

(From Aside) No question of that; for I have seen him whipped three market-days together.

Cade

I fear neither sword nor fire.

Smith

(From Aside) He need not fear the sword; for his coat is of proof.

Dick

(From Aside) But methinks he should stand in fear of fire, being burnt in the hand for stealing of sheep.

Cade

Be brave, then; for your captain is brave, and vows reformation. There shall be in England seven halfpenny loaves sold for a penny: the three-hooped pot shall have ten hoops and I will make it felony to drink small beer

All the realm shall be in common and in Cheapside shall my palfrey go to grass

When I am king, as king I will be...

All

God save your majesty!

Cade

I thank you, good people, there shall be no money

All shall eat and drink on my score

I will apparel them all in one livery, that they may agree like brothers and worship me their lord.

Dick

The first thing we do, let's kill all the lawyers.

Cade

Nay, that I mean to do. Is not this a lamentable thing, that of the skin of an innocent lamb should be made parchment?

That parchment, being scribbled over, should undo a man?

Some say the bee stings, but I say this the bee's wax; for I did but seal once to a thing, and I was never mine own man since.

How now! who's there?

(Some enter, bringing forward the Clerk of Chatham)

Smith

(The clerk of Chatham, he can write and read and cast accompt)

Cade

Oh monstrous!

Smith

We took him setting of boys' copies.

Cade

Here's a villain!

Smith

Has a book in his pocket with red letters in it.

Cade

Nay, then, he is a conjurer.

Dick

Nay, he can make obligations, and write court-hand.

Cade

I am sorry for it, the man is a proper man, of mine honour

Unless I find him guilty, he shall not die.

Come hither, sirrah, I must examine thee: what is thy name?

Clerk

Emmanuel.

Dick

They use to write it on the top of letters, it will go hard with you.

Cade

Let me alone.

Dost thou use to write thy name?

Or hast thou a mark to thyself, like an honest plain-dealing man?

Clerk

Sir, I thank God, I have been so well brought up that I can write my name.

All

He hath confessed: away with him! he's a villain and a traitor.

Cade

Away with him, I say! hang him with his pen and ink-horn about his neck.

(Exit with the Clerk)

(Michael enters)

Michael

Where's our general?

Cade

Here I am, thou particular fellow.

Michael

Fly, fly, fly! Sir Humphrey Stafford and his brother are hard by, with the king's forces.

Cade

Stand, villain, stand, or I'll fell thee down.

He shall be encountered with a man as good as himself, he is but a knight, is a?

Michael

No.

Cade

To equal him, I will make myself a knight presently.

(Kneels)

Rise up Sir John Mortimer.

(Rises)

Now have at him!

(Sir Humphrey and William Stafford, with drum and soldiers enter)

Sir Humphrey

Rebellious hinds, the filth and scum of Kent marked for the gallows, lay your weapons down

Home to your cottages, forsake this groom, the king is merciful, if you revolt.

William Stafford

But angry, wrathful, and inclined to blood, if you go forward

Yield, or die.

Cade

As for these silken-coated slaves, I pass not, it is to you good people that I speak, over whom in time to come I hope to reign

For I am rightful heir unto the crown.

Sir Humphrey

Villain, thy father was a plasterer

Thou thyself a shearman, art thou not?

Cade

And Adam was a gardener.

William Stafford

And what of that?

Cade

Marry, this: Edmund Mortimer, Earl of March.

Married the Duke of Clarence' daughter, did he not?

Sir Humphrey

Ay, sir.

Cade

By her he had two children at one birth.

William Stafford

That's false.

Cade

Ay, there's the question; but I say it is true, the elder of them, being put to nurse was by a beggar-woman stolen away

Ignorant of his birth and parentage, became a bricklayer when he came to age, his son am I

Deny it, if you can.

Dick

Nay, it is too true

He shall be king.

Smith

Sir, he made a chimney in my father's house, and the bricks are alive at this day to testify it

Deny it not.

Sir Humphrey

And will you credit this base drudge's words, that speaks he knows not what?

All

Ay, marry, will we

Get ye gone.

William Stafford

Jack Cade, the Duke of York hath taught you this.

Cade

(From Aside) He lies, for I invented it myself.

Go to, sirrah, tell the king from me, that, for his father's sake, Henry the Fifth in whose time boys went to span-counter for French crowns

I am content he shall reign, but I'll be protector over him.

Dick

And furthermore, well have the Lord Say's head for selling the dukedom of Maine.

Cade

And good reason

Thereby is England mained and fain to go with a staff, but that my puissance holds it up.

Fellow kings, I tell you that that Lord say hath gelded the commonwealth, and made it an eunuch, and more than that he can speak French

Therefore he is a traitor.

Sir Humphrey

Oh gross and miserable ignorance!

Cade

Nay, answer, if you can, the Frenchmen are our enemies

Go to, then, I ask but this, can he that speaks with the tongue of an enemy be a good counsellor, or no?

All

No, no; and therefore we'll have his head.

William Stafford

Well, seeing gentle words will not prevail, assail them with the army of the king.

Sir Humphrey

Herald, away

Throughout every town proclaim them traitors that are up with Cade

That those which fly before the battle ends may, even in their wives' and children's sight be hang'd up for example at their doors

And you that be the king's friends, follow me.

(William Stafford, Sir Humphrey, and soldiers exit)

Cade

And you that love the commons, follow me.

Now show yourselves men

It is for liberty.

We will not leave one lord, one gentleman, spare none but such as go in clouted shoon

They are thrifty honest men, and such as would, but that they dare not, take our parts.

Dick

They are all in order and march toward us.

Cade

But then are we in order when we are most out of order. Come, march forward.

(Exit)

Act 4 Scene 3

Another part of Blackheath.

(Alarums to the fight)

(Sir Humphrey and William Stafford are slain.

(Cade and the rest enter)

Cade

Where's Dick, the butcher of Ashford?

Dick

Here, sir.

Cade

They fell before thee like sheep and oxen, and thou behavedst thyself as if thou hadst been in thine own slaughter-house, therefore thus will I reward thee, the Lent shall be as long again as it is

Thou shalt have a licence to kill for a hundred lacking one.

Dick

I desire no more.

Cade

And, to speak truth, thou deservest no less.

This monument of the victory will I bear

(Putting on Sir Humphrey's brigandine)

The bodies shall be dragged at my horse' heels till I do come to London, where we will have the mayor's sword borne before us.

Dick

If we mean to thrive and do good, break open the goals and let out the prisoners.

Cade

Fear not that, I warrant thee. Come, let's march towards London.

(Exit)

Act 4 Scene 4

London. The palace.

(King Henry VI enters with a supplication, and the Queen with Suffolk's head, Buckingham and Lord Say)

Queen Margaret

Often have I heard that grief softens the mind, and makes it fearful and degenerate

Think therefore on revenge and cease to weep.

But who can cease to weep and look on this?

Here may his head lie on my throbbing breast, but where's the body that I should embrace?

Buckingham

What answer makes your grace to the rebels' supplication?

King Henry VI

I'll send some holy bishop to entreat

For God forbid so many simple souls should perish by the sword! And I myself rather than bloody war shall cut them short will parley with Jack Cade their general, but stay I'll read it over once again.

Queen Margaret

Ah, barbarous villains! hath this lovely face ruled, like a wandering planet, over me, and could it not enforce them to relent that were unworthy to behold the same?

King Henry VI

Lord Say, Jack Cade hath sworn to have thy head.

Say

Ay, but I hope your highness shall have his.

King Henry VI

How now, madam!

Still lamenting and mourning for Suffolk's death?

I fear me, love, if that I had been dead, thou wouldst not have mourned so much for me.

Queen Margaret

No, my love, I should not mourn, but die for thee.

(A Messenger enters)

King Henry VI

How now! what news? why comest thou in such haste?

Messenger

The rebels are in Southwark

Fly, my lord!

Jack Cade proclaims himself Lord Mortimer, descended from the Duke of Clarence' house and calls your grace usurper openly, and vows to crown himself in Westminster.

His army is a ragged multitude of hinds and peasants, rude and merciless, Sir Humphrey Stafford and his brother's death hath given them heart and courage to proceed

All scholars, lawyers, courtiers, gentlemen, they call false caterpillars and intend their death.

King Henry VI

Oh graceless men! they know not what they do.

Buckingham

My gracious lord, return to Killingworth until a power be raised to put them down.

Queen Margaret

Ah, were the Duke of Suffolk now alive, these Kentish rebels would be soon appeased!

King Henry VI

Lord Say, the traitors hate thee

Away with us to Killingworth.

Say

So might your grace's person be in danger.

The sight of me is odious in their eyes

Therefore in this city will I stay and live alone as secret as I may.

(Another Messenger enters)

Messenger

Jack Cade hath gotten London bridge

The citizens fly and forsake their houses, the rascal people, thirsting after prey, join with the traitor, and they jointly swear to spoil the city and your royal court.

Buckingham

Then linger not, my lord, away, take horse.

King Henry VI

Come, Margaret; God, our hope, will succor us.

Queen Margaret

My hope is gone, now Suffolk is deceased.

King Henry VI

Farewell, my lord: trust not the Kentish rebels.

Buckingham

Trust nobody, for fear you be betrayed.

Say

The trust I have is in mine innocence, and therefore am I bold and resolute.

(Exit)

Act 4 Scene 5

London. The Tower.

(Scales enters upon the Tower, walking.

(Then two or three Citizens enter below)

Scales

How now! is Jack Cade slain?

First Citizen

No, my lord, nor likely to be slain

They have won the bridge, killing all those that withstand them, the lord mayor craves aid of your honour from the Tower, to defend the city from the rebels.

Scales

Such aid as I can spare you shall command

I am troubled here with them myself

The rebels have assayed to win the Tower.

But get you to Smithfield, and gather head, and thither I will send you Matthew Goffe

Fight for your king, your country and your lives

And so, farewell, for I must hence again.

(Exit)

Act 4 Scene 6

London. Cannon Street.

(Cade and the rest enter, and strikes his staff on London-stone)

Cade

Now is Mortimer lord of this city.

And here, sitting upon London-stone, I charge and command that of the city's cost, the pissing-conduit run nothing but claret wine this first year of our reign.

And now henceforward it shall be treason for any that calls me other than Lord Mortimer.

(A Soldier enters, running)

Soldier

Jack Cade! Jack Cade!

Cade

Knock him down there.

(They kill him)

Smith

If this fellow be wise, he'll never call ye Jack Cade more, I think he hath a very fair warning.

Dick

My lord, there's an army gathered together in Smithfield.

Cade

Come, then, let's go fight with them; but first, go and set London bridge on fire

If you can, burn down the Tower too. Come, let's away.

(Exit)

Act 4 Scene 7

London. Smithfield.

(Alarums)

(Matthew Goffe is slain, and all the rest)

(Then Cade enters with his company)

Cade

So, sirs, now go some and pull down the Savoy

Others to the inns of court

Down with them all.

Dick

I have a suit unto your lordship.

Cade

Be it a lordship, thou shalt have it for that word.

Dick

Only that the laws of England may come out of your mouth.

Holland

(From Aside) Mass, it will be sore law, then

He was thrust in the mouth with a spear, and it is not whole yet.

Smith

(**From Aside**) Nay, John, it will be stinking law for his breath stinks with eating toasted cheese.

Cade

I have thought upon it, it shall be so.

Away, burn all the records of the realm: my mouth shall be the parliament of England.

Holland

(**From Aside**) Then we are like to have biting statutes, unless his teeth be pulled out.

Cade

And henceforward all things shall be in common.

(A Messenger enters)

Messenger

My lord, a prize, a prize! here's the Lord Say, which sold the towns in France

He that made us pay one and twenty fifteens, and one shilling to the pound, the last subsidy.

(Bevis enters, with Lord Say)

Cade

Well, he shall be beheaded for it ten times.

Ah, thou say, thou serge, nay thou buckram lord!

Now art thou within point-blank of our jurisdiction regal.

What canst thou answer to my majesty for giving up of Normandy unto Mounsieur Basimecu, the dauphin of France?

Be it known unto thee by these presence, even the presence of Lord Mortimer, that I am the besom that must sweep the court clean of such filth as thou art.

Thou hast most traitorously corrupted the youth of the realm in erecting a grammar school

Whereas, before, our forefathers had no other books but the score and the tally, thou hast caused printing to be used, and contrary to the king, his crown and dignity, thou hast built a paper-mill.

It will be proved to thy face that thou hast men about thee that usually talk of a noun and a verb, and such abominable words as no Christian ear can endure to hear.

Thou hast appointed justices of peace, to call poor men before them about matters they were not able to answer.

Moreover, thou hast put them in prison; and because they could not read, thou hast hanged them; when, indeed, only for that cause they have been most worthy to live.

Thou dost ride in a foot-cloth, dost thou not?

Say

What of that?

Cade

Marry, thou oughtest not to let thy horse wear a cloak, when honester men than thou go in their hose and doublets.

Dick

And work in their shirt too

As myself, for example, that am a butcher.

Say

You men of Kent...

Dick

What say you of Kent?

Say

Nothing but this; it is a good country, with horrible people

Cade

Away with him, away with him! he speaks a Latin saying.

Say

Hear me but speak, and bear me where you will.

Kent, in the Commentaries Caesar writ,

Is termed the civil'st place of this isle, sweet is the country, because full of riches

The people liberal, valiant, active, wealthy

Which makes me hope you are not void of pity.

I sold not Maine, I lost not Normandy, yet to recover them would lose my life.

Justice with favour have I always done

Prayers and tears have moved me, gifts could never.

When have I aught exacted at your hands but to maintain the king, the realm and you?

Large gifts have I bestowed on learned clerks because my book preferred me to the king, and seeing ignorance is the curse of God, Knowledge the wing wherewith we fly to heaven unless you be possessed with devilish spirits,

You cannot but forbear to murder me, this tongue hath spoken unto foreign kings, for your behalf...

Cade

Tut, when struck'st thou one blow in the field?

Say

Great men have reaching hands, often have I struck those that I never saw and struck them dead.

Bevis

Oh monstrous coward! what, to come behind folks?

Say

These cheeks are pale for watching for your good.

Cade

Give him a box on the ear and that will make them red again.

Say

Long sitting to determine poor men's causes hath made me full of sickness and diseases.

Cade

Ye shall have a hempen caudle, then, and the help of hatchet.

Dick

Why dost thou quiver, man?

Say

The palsy, and not fear, provokes me.

Cade

Nay, he nods at us, as who should say, I'll be even with you, I'll see if his head will stand steadier on a pole, or no.

Take him away, and behead him.

Say

Tell me wherein have I offended most?

Have I affected wealth or honour? speak.

Are my chests fill'd up with extorted gold?

Is my apparel sumptuous to behold?

Whom have I injured, that ye seek my death?

These hands are free from guiltless bloodshedding, this breast from harbouring foul deceitful thoughts.

Oh let me live!

Cade

(From Aside) I feel remorse in myself with his words

I'll bridle it, he shall die and it be but for pleading so well for his life.

Away with him!

He has a familiar under his tongue; he speaks not of God's name.

Go, take him away, I say, and strike off his head presently

Then break into his son-in-law's house, Sir James Cromer, and strike off his head, and bring them both upon two poles hither.

All

It shall be done.

Say

Ah, countrymen! if when you make your prayers, God should be so obdurate as yourselves, how would it fare with your departed souls?

And therefore yet relent, and save my life.

Cade

Away with him! and do as I command ye.

(Some exit with Lord Say)

The proudest peer in the realm shall not wear a head on his shoulders, unless he pay me tribute

There shall not a maid be married, but she shall pay to me her maidenhead ere they have it, men shall hold of me in capite

We charge and command that their wives be as free as heart can wish or tongue can tell.

Dick

My lord, when shall we go to Cheapside and take up commodities upon our bills?

Cade

Marry, presently.

All

Oh brave!

(Re-enters one with the heads)

Cade

But is not this braver?

Let them kiss one another, for they loved well when they were alive.

Now part them again, lest they consult about the giving up of some more towns in France.

Soldiers, defer the spoil of the city until night: for with these borne before us, instead of maces, will we ride through the streets, and at every corner have them kiss. Away!

(Exit)

Act 4 Scene 8

Southwark.

(Alarum and retreat)

(Cade enters and all his rabblement)

Cade

Up Fish Street! down Saint Magnus' Corner!

Kill and knock down! throw them into Thames!

Sound a meeting

What noise is this I hear?

Dare any be so bold to sound retreat or meeting, when I command them kill?

(Buckingham and Clifford enter, attended)

Buckingham

Ay, here they be that dare and will disturb thee, know Cade, we come ambassadors from the king unto the commons whom thou hast misled

Here pronounce free pardon to them all that will forsake thee and go home in peace.

Clifford

What say ye, countrymen? will ye relent, and yield to mercy whilst it is offered you or let a rebel lead you to your deaths?

Who loves the king and will embrace his pardon, fling up his cap, and say God save his majesty!

Who hateth him and honours not his father, Henry the Fifth, that made all France to quake, Shake he his weapon at us and pass by.

All

God save the king! God save the king!

Cade

What, Buckingham and Clifford, are ye so brave?

And you, base peasants, do ye believe him?

Will you needs be hanged with your pardons about your necks?

Hath my sword therefore broke through London gates, that you should leave me at the White Hart in Southwark?

I thought ye would never have given out these arms till you had recovered your ancient freedom, but you are all recreants and dastards, and delight to live in slavery to the nobility.

Let them break your backs with burthens, take your houses over your heads, ravish your wives and daughters before your faces

For me, I will make shift for one

So, God's curse light upon you all!

All

We'll follow Cade, we'll follow Cade!

Clifford

Is Cade the son of Henry the Fifth, that thus you do exclaim you'll go with him?

Will he conduct you through the heart of France and make the meanest of you earls and dukes?

Alas, he hath no home, no place to fly to

Nor knows he how to live but by the spoil unless by robbing of your friends and us.

Were it not a shame, that whilst you live at jar, the fearful French, whom you late vanquished should make a start over seas and vanquish you?

Methinks already in this civil broil I see them lording it in London streets, crying Villiago! unto all they meet.

Better ten thousand base-born Cades miscarry than you should stoop unto a Frenchman's mercy.

To France, to France, and get what you have lost

Spare England, for it is your native coast

Henry hath money, you are strong and manly

God on our side, doubt not of victory.

All

A Clifford! a Clifford! we'll follow the king and Clifford.

Cade

Was ever feather so lightly blown to and fro as this multitude?

The name of Henry the Fifth hales them to an hundred mischiefs, and makes them leave me desolate.

I see them lay their heads together to surprise me.

My sword make way for me, for here is no staying.

In despite of the devils and hell, have through the very middest of you? and heavens and honour be witness, that no want of resolution in me.

But only my followers' base and ignominious treasons, makes me betake me to my heels.

(Exit)

Buckingham

What, is he fled? Go some, and follow him

And he that brings his head unto the king shall have a thousand crowns for his reward.

(Some of them exit)

Follow me, soldiers, we'll devise a mean to reconcile you all unto the king. **(Exit)**

Act 4 Scene 9

Kenilworth Castle.

(Sound Trumpets)

(King Henry VI, Queen Margaret, and Somerset enter, on the terrace)

King Henry VI

Was ever king that joyed an earthly throne, and could command no more content than I?

No sooner was I crept out of my cradle but I was made a king, at nine months old.

Was never subject longed to be a king as I do long and wish to be a subject.

(Buckingham and Clifford enter)

Buckingham

Health and glad tidings to your majesty!

King Henry VI

Why, Buckingham, is the traitor Cade surprised?

Or is he but retired to make him strong?

(Below, multitudes enter with halters about their necks)

Clifford

He is fled, my lord, and all his powers do yield

Humbly thus, with halters on their necks, expect your highness' doom of life or death.

King Henry VI

Then, heaven, set ope thy everlasting gates, to entertain my vows of thanks and praise!

Soldiers, this day have you redeemed your lives, and showed how well you love your prince and country, continue still in this so good a mind, and Henry though he be infortunate

Assure yourselves, will never be unkind, and so with thanks and pardon to you all, I do dismiss you to your several countries.

All

God save the king! God save the king!

(A Messenger enter)

Messenger

Please it your grace to be advertised the Duke of York is newly come from Ireland, and with a puissant and a mighty power of gallowglasses and stout kerns is marching hitherward in proud array, and still proclaimeth, as he comes along

His arms are only to remove from thee the Duke of Somerset, whom he terms traitor.

King Henry VI

Thus stands my state, 'twixt Cade and York distressed.

Like to a ship that, having escaped a tempest, is straightway calmed and boarded with a pirate

But now is Cade driven back, his men dispersed

Now is York in arms to second him.

I pray thee, Buckingham, go and meet him and ask him what's the reason of these arms.

Tell him I'll send Duke Edmund to the Tower

And, Somerset, we'll commit thee thither until his army be dismissed from him.

Somerset

My lord, I'll yield myself to prison willingly or unto death, to do my country good.

King Henry VI

In any case, be not too rough in terms

For he is fierce and cannot brook hard language.

Buckingham

I will, my lord; and doubt not so to deal as all things shall redound unto your good.

King Henry VI

Come, wife, let's in, and learn to govern better

For yet may England curse my wretched reign.

(Flourish)

(Exit)

Act 4 Scene 10

Kent. Iden's garden.

(**Cade enters**)

Cade

Fie on ambition! fire on myself, that have a sword, and yet am ready to famish!

These five days have I hid me in these woods and durst not peep out, for all the country is laid for me

Now am I so hungry that if I might have a lease of my life for a thousand years I could stay no longer.

Wherefore, on a brick wall have I climbed into this garden, to see if I can eat grass, or pick a sallet another while, which is not amiss to cool a man's stomach this hot weather.

I think this word sallet was born to do me good: for many a time, but for a sallet, my brainpan had been cleft with a brown bill

Many a time, when I have been dry and bravely marching, it hath served me instead of a quart pot to drink in; and now the word sallet must serve me to feed on.

(**Iden enters**)

Iden

Lord, who would live turmoiled in the court, and may enjoy such quiet walks as these?

This small inheritance my father left me contenteth me, and worth a monarchy.

I seek not to wax great by others' waning, or gather wealth, I care not, with what envy sufficeth that I have maintains my state and sends the poor well pleased from my gate.

Cade

Here's the lord of the soil come to seize me for a stray, for entering his fee-simple without leave.

Ah, villain, thou wilt betray me, and get a thousand crowns of the king carrying my head to him, but I'll make thee eat iron like an ostrich, and swallow my sword like a great pin, ere thou and I part.

Iden

Why, rude companion, whatsoever thou be, I know thee not; why, then, should I betray thee?

Is it not enough to break into my garden, and, like a thief, to come to rob my grounds, climbing my walls in spite of me the owner, but thou wilt brave me with these saucy terms?

Cade

Brave thee! ay, by the best blood that ever was broached, and beard thee too.

Look on me well, I have eat no meat these five days; yet, come thou and thy five men, and if I do not leave you all as dead as a doornail

I pray God I may never eat grass more.

Iden

Nay, it shall never be said, while England stands that Alexander Iden, an esquire of Kent, took odds to combat a poor famished man.

Oppose thy steadfast-gazing eyes to mine, see if thou canst outface me with thy looks

Set limb to limb, and thou art far the lesser

Thy hand is but a finger to my fist, thy leg a stick compared with this truncheon

My foot shall fight with all the strength thou hast

If mine arm be heaved in the air, thy grave is diggd already in the earth.

As for words, whose greatness answers words, let this my sword report what speech forbears.

Cade

By my valour, the most complete champion that ever I heard!

Steel, if thou turn the edge, or cut not out the burly-boned clown in chines of beef were thou sleep in thy sheath, I beseech God on my knees thou mayst be turned to hobnails.

(They fight, Cade falls)

Oh, I am slain! famine and no other hath slain me

Let ten thousand devils come against me, and give me but the ten meals I have lost, and I'll defy them all.

Wither, garden; and be henceforth a burying-place to all that do dwell in this house, because the unconquered soul of Cade is fled.

Iden

Is it Cade that I have slain, that monstrous traitor?

Sword, I will hollow thee for this thy deed and hang thee o'er my tomb when I am dead

Never shall this blood be wiped from thy point

Thou shalt wear it as a herald's coat to emblaze the honour that thy master got.

Cade

Iden, farewell, and be proud of thy victory.

Tell Kent from me, she hath lost her best man, and exhort all the world to be cowards

For I, that never feared any, am vanquished by famine, not by valour.

(Dies)

Iden

How much thou wrong'st me, heaven be my judge.

Die, damned wretch, the curse of her that bare thee

As I thrust thy body in with my sword, so wish I, I might thrust thy soul to hell.

Hence will I drag thee headlong by the heels unto a dunghill which shall be thy grave and there cut off thy most ungracious head, which I will bear in triumph to the king, leaving thy trunk for crows to feed upon

(Exit)

Act 5 Scene 1

Fields between Dartford and Blackheath.

(York and his army of Irish enter, with drum and colours)

York

From Ireland thus comes York to claim his right, and pluck the crown from feeble Henry's head

Ring, bells, aloud

Burn, bonfires, clear and bright to entertain great England's lawful king

Ah! Sacred Majesty, who would not buy thee dear?

Let them obey that know not how to rule

This hand was made to handle naught but gold.

I cannot give due action to my words, except a sword or sceptre balance it

A sceptre shall it have, have I a soul, on which I'll toss the flower-de-luce of France.

(Buckingham enters)

Whom have we here? Buckingham, to disturb me?

The king hath sent him, sure, I must dissemble.

Buckingham

York, if thou meanest well, I greet thee well.

York

Humphrey of Buckingham, I accept thy greeting.

Art thou a messenger, or come of pleasure?

Buckingham

A messenger from Henry, our dread liege, to know the reason of these arms in peace

Why thou, being a subject as I am, against thy oath and true allegiance sworn should raise so great a power without his leave, or dare to bring thy force so near the court.

York

(From Aside) Scarce can I speak, my choler is so great

Oh, I could hew up rocks and fight with flint, I am so angry at these abject terms

And now, like Ajax Telamonius, on sheep or oxen could I spend my fury.

I am far better born than is the king, more like a king, more kingly in my thoughts, but I must make fair weather yet a while, till Henry be more weak and I more strong...

Buckingham, I pray to thee, pardon me, that I have given no answer all this while

My mind was troubled with deep melancholy.

The cause why I have brought this army hither is to remove proud Somerset from the king, seditious to his grace and to the state.

Buckingham

That is too much presumption on thy part, but if thy arms be to no other end, the king hath yielded unto thy demand

The Duke of Somerset is in the Tower.

York

Upon thine honour, is he prisoner?

Buckingham

Upon mine honour, he is prisoner.

York

Then, Buckingham, I do dismiss my powers.

Soldiers, I thank you all; disperse yourselves

Meet me to-morrow in St. George's field, you shall have pay and everything you wish.

And let my sovereign, virtuous Henry, command my eldest son, nay, all my sons, as pledges of my fealty and love

I'll send them all as willing as I live, lands, goods, horse, armour, anything I have, is his to use, so Somerset may die.

Buckingham

York, I commend this kind submission, we twain will go into his highness' tent.

(King Henry VI and Attendants enter)

King Henry VI

Buckingham, doth York intend no harm to us, that thus he marcheth with thee arm in arm?

York

In all submission and humility York doth present himself unto your highness.

King Henry VI

Then what intends these forces thou dost bring?

York

To heave the traitor Somerset from hence, and fight against that monstrous rebel Cade, who since I heard to be discomfited.

(Iden enters with Cade's head)

Iden

If one so rude and of so mean condition may pass into the presence of a king, Lord I present your grace a traitor's head, the head of Cade, whom I in combat slew.

King Henry VI

The head of Cade! Great God, how just art Thou!

Oh, let me view his visage, being dead, that living wrought me such exceeding trouble.

Tell me, my friend, art thou the man that slew him?

Iden

I was, and it like your majesty.

King Henry VI

How art thou called? and what is thy degree?

Iden

Alexander Iden, that's my name

Poor esquire of Kent, that loves his king.

Buckingham

So please it you, my lord, it were not amiss he were created knight for his good service.

King Henry VI

Iden, kneel down.

(He kneels)

Rise up a knight.

We give thee for reward a thousand marks, and will that thou henceforth attend on us.

Iden

May Iden live to merit such a bounty and never live but true unto his liege!

(Rises)

(Queen Margaret and **Somerset enter)**

King Henry VI

See, Buckingham, Somerset comes with the queen

Go, bid her hide him quickly from the duke.

Queen Margaret

For thousand Yorks he shall not hide his head, but boldly stand and front him to his face.

York

How now! is Somerset at liberty?

Then, York, unloose thy long-imprisoned thoughts, and let thy tongue be equal with thy heart.

Shall I endure the sight of Somerset?

False king! why hast thou broken faith with me, knowing how hardly I can brook abuse?

King did I call thee? no, thou art not king, not fit to govern and rule multitudes, which darest not, no, nor canst not rule a traitor.

That head of thine doth not become a crown

Thy hand is made to grasp a palmer's staff and not to grace an awful princely sceptre.

That gold must round engirt these brows of mine whose smile and frown, like to Achilles' spear, is able with the change to kill and cure.

Here is a hand to hold a sceptre up and with the same to act controlling laws.

Give place, by heaven, thou shalt rule no more over him whom heaven created for thy ruler.

Somerset

Oh monstrous traitor! I arrest thee York, of capital treason against the king and crown

Obey, audacious traitor; kneel for grace.

York

Wouldst have me kneel? first let me ask of these, if they can brook I bow a knee to man.

Sirrah, call in my sons to be my bail;

(Attendant exits)

I know, ere they will have me go to ward, they'll pawn their swords for my enfranchisement.

Queen Margaret

Call hither Clifford! bid him come amain, to say if that the bastard boys of York shall be the surety for their traitor father.

(Buckingham exits)

York

Oh blood-besotted Neapolitan, outcast of Naples, England's bloody scourge!

The sons of York, thy betters in their birth shall be their father's bail

Bane to those that for my surety will refuse the boys!

(Edward and Richard enter)

See where they come, I'll warrant they'll make it good.

(Clifford and Young Clifford enter)

Queen Margaret

And here comes Clifford to deny their bail.

Clifford

Health and all happiness to my lord the king!

(Kneels)

York

I thank thee, Clifford

Say, what news with thee?

Nay, do not fright us with an angry look

We are thy sovereign, Clifford, kneel again

For thy mistaking so, we pardon thee.

Clifford

This is my king, York, I do not mistake

Thou mistakest me much to think I do, to Bedlam with him! is the man grown mad?

King Henry VI

Ay, Clifford

A bedlam and ambitious humour makes him oppose himself against his king.

Clifford

He is a traitor; let him to the Tower and chop away that factious pate of his.

Queen Margaret

He is arrested, but will not obey

His sons, he says, shall give their words for him.

York

Will you not, sons?

Edward

Ay, noble father, if our words will serve.

Richard

And if words will not, then our weapons shall.

Clifford

Why, what a brood of traitors have we here!

York

Look in a glass, and call thy image so, I am thy king, and thou a false-heart traitor.

Call hither to the stake my two brave bears, that with the very shaking of their chains they may astonish these fell-lurking curs

Bid Salisbury and Warwick come to me.

(Warwick and Salisbury enter)

Clifford

Are these thy bears? we'll bait thy bears to death.

And manacle the bear-ward in their chains, if thou darest bring them to the baiting place.

Richard

Often have I seen a hot overweening cur, run back and bite because he was withheld

Being suffered with the bear's fell paw hath clapped his tail between his legs and cried, and such a piece of service will you do, if you oppose yourselves to match Lord Warwick.

Clifford

Hence, heap of wrath, foul indigested lump, as crooked in thy manners as thy shape!

York

Nay, we shall heat you thoroughly anon.

Clifford

Take heed, lest by your heat you burn yourselves.

King Henry VI

Why, Warwick, hath thy knee forgot to bow?

Old Salisbury, shame to thy silver hair, thou mad misleader of thy brain-sick son!

What, wilt thou on thy death-bed play the ruffian and seek for sorrow with thy spectacles?

Oh where is faith? Oh where is loyalty?

If it be banished from the frosty head, where shall it find a harbour in the earth?

Wilt thou go dig a grave to find out war and shame thine honourable age with blood?

Why art thou old, and want'st experience?

Or wherefore dost abuse it, if thou hast it?

For shame! in duty bend thy knee to me that bows unto the grave with mickle age.

Salisbury

My lord, I have considered with myself the title of this most renowned duke

In my conscience do repute his grace the rightful heir to England's royal seat.

King Henry VI

Hast thou not sworn allegiance unto me?

Salisbury

I have.

King Henry VI

Canst thou dispense with heaven for such an oath?

Salisbury

It is great sin to swear unto a sin, but greater sin to keep a sinful oath.

Who can be bound by any solemn vow to do a murderous deed, to rob a man, to force a spotless virgin's chastity, to reave the orphan of his patrimony to wring the widow from her customed right, and have no other reason for this wrong, but that he was bound by a solemn oath?

Queen Margaret

A subtle traitor needs no sophister.

King Henry VI

Call Buckingham, and bid him arm himself.

York

Call Buckingham, and all the friends thou hast, I am resolved for death or dignity.

Clifford

The first I warrant thee, if dreams prove true.

Warwick

You were best to go to bed and dream again, to keep thee from the tempest of the field.

Clifford

I am resolved to bear a greater storm than any thou canst conjure up to-day

That I'll write upon thy burgonet might I but know thee by thy household badge.

Warwick

Now, by my father's badge, old Nevil's crest, the rampant bear chained to the ragged staff, this day I'll wear aloft my burgonet as on a mountain top the cedar shows that keeps his leaves in spite of any storm, even to affright thee with the view thereof.

Clifford

And from thy burgonet I'll rend thy bear and tread it under foot with all contempt despite the bear-ward that protects the bear.

Young Clifford

And so to arms, victorious father, to quell the rebels and their complices

Richard

Fie! charity, for shame! speak not in spite, for you shall sup with Jesus Christ to-night.

Young Clifford

Foul stigmatic, that's more than thou canst tell.

Richard

If not in heaven, you'll surely sup in hell.

(Exits severally)

Act 5 Scene 2

Saint Alban's.

(Alarums to the battle)

(Warwick enters)

Warwick

Clifford of Cumberland, 'tis Warwick calls

If thou dost not hide thee from the bear, now, when the angry trumpet sounds alarum and dead men's cries do fill the empty air,

Clifford, I say, come forth and fight with me

Proud northern lord, Clifford of Cumberland, Warwick is hoarse with calling thee to arms.

(York enters)

How now, my noble lord? what, all afoot?

York

The deadly-handed Clifford slew my steed, but match to match I have encountered him and made a prey for carrion kites and crows even of the bonny beast he loved so well.

(Clifford enters)

Warwick

Of one or both of us the time is come.

York

Hold, Warwick, seek thee out some other chase, for I myself must hunt this deer to death.

Warwick

Then, nobly, York

It is for a crown thou fight'st.

As I intend, Clifford, to thrive to-day, it grieves my soul to leave thee unassailed.

(Exit)

Clifford

What seest thou in me, York? why dost thou pause?

York

With thy brave bearing should I be in love, but that thou art so fast mine enemy.

Clifford

Nor should thy prowess want praise and esteem, but that 'tis shown ignobly and in treason.

York

So let it help me now against thy sword as I in justice and true right express it.

Clifford

My soul and body on the action both!

York

A dreadful lay! Address thee instantly.

(They fight, and Clifford falls)

Clifford

The end crowns thy good works

(Dies)

York

Thus war hath given thee peace, for thou art still.

Peace with his soul, heaven, if it be thy will!

(Exit)

(Young Clifford enters)

Young Clifford

Shame and confusion! all is on the rout

Fear frames disorder, and disorder wounds where it should guard.

Oh war, thou son of hell, whom angry heavens do make their minister throw in the frozen bosoms of our part hot coals of vengeance!

Let no soldier fly.

He that is truly dedicate to war hath no self-love, nor he that loves himself hath not essentially but by circumstance the name of valour.

(Seeing his dead father)

Oh, let the vile world end, and the premised flames of the last day knit earth and heaven together!

Now let the general trumpet blow his blast, particularities and petty sounds to cease!

Was thou ordained, dear father, to lose thy youth in peace, and to achieve the silver livery of advised age, and in thy reverence and thy chair-days, thus to die in ruffian battle?

Even at this sight my heart is turned to stone, and while it is mine it shall be stony.

York not our old men spares

No more will I their babes, tears virginal shall be to me even as the dew to fire and beauty that the tyrant often reclaims shall to my flaming wrath be oil and flax.

Henceforth I will not have to do with pity, meet I an infant of the house of York into as many gobbets will I cut it as wild Medea young Absyrtus did

In cruelty will I seek out my fame. come thou new ruin of old Clifford's house, as did Aeneas old Anchises bear, so bear I thee upon my manly shoulders

Then Aeneas bare a living load, nothing so heavy as these woes of mine.

(Exits bearing off his father)

(Richard and Somerset fight. Somerset is killed)

Richard

So, lie thou there

For underneath an alehouse' paltry sign, the Castle in Saint Alban's, Somerset hath made the wizard famous in his death. sword, hold thy temper

Heart, be wrathful still, priests pray for enemies, but princes kill.

(Exit)

(Fights)

(Excursions)

(King Henry VI, Queen Margaret, and others enter)

Queen Margaret

Away, my lord! you are slow

For shame, away!

King Henry VI

Can we outrun the heavens? good Margaret, stay.

Queen Margaret

What are you made of? you'll nor fight nor fly, now is it manhood, wisdom and defence to give the enemy way and to secure us by what we can, which can no more but fly.

(Alarum afar off)

If you be taken, we then should see the bottom of all our fortunes, but if we haply scape as well we may, if not through your neglect we shall to London get where you are loved, and where this breach now in our fortunes made may readily be stopped.

(Young Clifford re-enters)

Young Clifford

But that my heart's on future mischief set, I would speak blasphemy ere bid you fly, but fly you must

Uncurable discomfit reigns in the hearts of all our present parts.

Away, for your relief! and we will live to see their day and them our fortune give, away my lord, away!

(Exit)

Act 5 Scene 3

Fields near St. Alban's

(Alarum)

(Retreat)

(York, Richard, Warwick, and Soldiers enter, with drum and colours)

York

Of Salisbury, who can report of him, that winter lion, who in rage forgets aged contusions and all brush of time like a gallant in the brow of youth, repairs him with occasion?

This happy day is not itself, nor have we won one foot if Salisbury be lost.

Richard

My noble father, three times to-day I help him to his horse, three times bestrid him

Thrice I led him off, persuaded him from any further act, but still, where danger was still there I met him

Like rich hangings in a homely house, so was his will in his old feeble body.

But, noble as he is, look where he comes.

(Salisbury enters)

Salisbury

Now, by my sword, well hast thou fought to-day

By the mass, so did we all. I thank you, Richard, God knows how long it is I have to live

It hath pleased him that three times to-day you have defended me from imminent death.

Well, lords, we have not got that which we have, it is not enough our foes are this time fled, being opposites of such repairing nature.

York

I know our safety is to follow them

For, as I hear, the king is fled to London to call a present court of parliament.

Let us pursue him ere the writs go forth.

What says Lord Warwick? shall we after them?

Warwick

After them! nay, before them, if we can.

Now, by my faith, lords, it was a glorious day, saint Alban's battle won by famous York shall be eternized in all age to come.

Sound drums and trumpets, and to London all, and more such days as these to us befall!

(Exit)   **The End**

Description of Titles

The Comedy of Errors
Caught in a land of embittered woman and war, caught in months of strife, where a merchant's visit offers little natural relief. The fleeting moment of approving gold, inspire further bitterness, upon an approach to the marketplace, and then the women that occupy within them.

19 Characters

The Taming of the Shrew
Arrangements are made to spencer would be suiters to melt the splendors of a strong willed women. The winning is found pledged, influencing maids to seek their turns, and meanwhile terms required, an authentic spirit that they will/would wed soon.

34 Characters

Love's Labor's Lost
The house of a scholarly pursuit, returns into an expressive, either poetic or drunken as highlighting the gold-slur filled house of charms and dance like rhymes

19 Characters

A Midsummer Night's Dream
Journey into a land of fairies, where creatures are found to have the same issues as nobilities. Exemplifying, perhaps, there's no place like home. Meet fairies as they frolic and play the noble hearts and sway, posed in the recesses of night, and mystic lands of a faraway kingdom.

22 Characters

The Merchant of Venice

An angry Shylock brings to trial a merchant, over a lover's quarrel disrupted, demanding pounds of flesh. With no desires for even three times the amount, the Shylock demands his vengeance at heart.

22 Characters

The Merry Wives of Windsor

Mistresses and lords try and relate towards one another, as various important community figures come to have their word/seek the hostesses. Pleasantries are exchanged as a range of charms are expressed, until conversation resembled so to folly.

23 Characters

Much Ado About Nothing

Soldiery level consideration occupy the gossip, as several hostilities are summoned up, onto heart related matter. Also in conflict. The latter portion of the story lightens up to a women's home and pleasantries. Thereafter, a general search and care in actions, creating response phrasing poetic to the responses of leadership parading, until an end full of sensitivity asking gently questions, onto kisses

23 Characters

As You Like It

Troubled lower nobles venture about daily business, with some mild graces towards the ladies found. In need of relief or play, the Duke and family members take to the woods, where jests of drinking turn into troubled amusements, or warmth of a women's heart.

26 Characters

Troilus and Cressida

The infamous Greek battle for Troy. A large army arrives to take back the lost love of a humiliated foe. Both sides mobilize heroes onto the field, as soldiers and generals move to the side, and let strategies and fate take their course.

21+ Characters

All's Well That Ends Well

A tale of delightful, womanly gossip of a prestigious sort, until the French King has his word on the excellence of others. The story initially revolves around a strong willed countess, whose courteous pose and insight, reflect a nobility reflective of the house and court (council). Dialogue therein revolving around the councils rather, to exemplify (court counselling women).

25 Characters

Measure for Measure

Statesmen discourse leading with time to a personal reflection. Strolling Dukes and strong willed women occupy the background, where high-function status and family discourse intertwine within formalities (of administrative foresight, expression) observed.

24 Characters

Richard III

An in palace drama with King Richard the 3rd, Queen Elizabeth, and Queen Margret. Onto a haunting reunion, as the state processes royal executions.

61+ Characters

The Life and Death of King John

King John and Queen Elinor entertain the royal court, where a bastard has come to make his day. Strategic deployments of influence are exemplified, as the bastard plots about until alerts, alarm corruption has delivered trouble makers known.

24 Characters

Romeo and Juliet

Lovers emerge within a city gripped with two feuding houses apposed. As turmoil are caught in bitter heat, the lover's. Bliss and undying pledge becomes them, onto the eternal soul (of love and romance).

33 Characters

Othello

A hopeful Othello calls upon the favor of allies based on proposed merits, which called upon allies and foes to him. In a mixed response, allies and foes campaign both against Othello, becoming a bitter, personal tangle over a mislead love adventure representing the future of either fates

25 Characters

Macbeth

A desperate Macbeth ventures towards witches to tell fortune, returning to a castle haunted by ghost/old-spirits. Macbeth's worries become frightful nightmares, along the despair of the household around him.

39 Characters

Mark Antony and Cleopatra

The relations or affections of Mark Anthony and Cleopatra, onto the strategic interactions between Mark Anthony and Octavius. The discourse moves to the Octavius house, revealing Octavia, and later then, Pompey in the background. Overall the focus retains upon Mark Anthony, Cleopatra, and Octavius.

56+ Characters

Coriolanus

Citizens riot during a famine, while the state administrative intervenes and otherwise discourses the seriousness of the matter and war. Lady's calm the general ambience, until the sword is mobilized to defend the gates, , while the plight of people is nevertheless heard convincing Roman elites the problem is being found/fought within.

60 Characters

Pericles Prince of Tyre

A thoughtful/reflective Pericles interposes his good will and well-meaning nature, which leads him to visit fishermen friends, and onto state function. Pericles is then confronted, required to (take a plunge) to marry, embedding him deeper into ocean stock of sea life among sailors experience and merchant owners, investing his interest as babe, securing his destiny as then, future king

44 Characters

Cymbeline

Cymbeline, friend or loyalist to the first Caesars, is summoned into battle. Meanwhile there are personal matters to attend to within the noble house.

41 Characters

The Winter's Tale

A gossipy tale of high office, administrative daily insight onto the tender meaning of things and people an how they unite unwittingly at the discourse of their respected hierarchies of partnership. Profoundness therein inspiring the recounts of clown and child, as examples perhaps of what state administration and or nobility's company keeps.

34+ Characters

The Tempest

After an earth shattering storm, a fairy dwelling world is found. There magic and graces are there in song, glory and praises.

21 Characters

The Two Gentlemen of Verona
Loving beginnings, yet far too. General virtues going upwards in hierarchies, with overall chivalrous wits.

Twelfth Night
An evening in the company of sound gatherings, seemingly a docile manner recount version of noble delights. In similarities of the pose, composing an environment of insight and oversight.

Henry the 8th
Across chamber and palace, Dukes and lords, until Queen Katharine's and King Henry VIII's present their graces, conversing the Cardinal then. The signs then, an Elizabeth is born.

Richard II
King Richard the 2nd readies the armed forces at the sound of alarm, while later Henry IV is near for discussion. King Richard the 2nd and his groom.

Henry V

King Henry the 5th, as found across his palace, until a readiness for war. King Henry the 5th and the French King, with armies both have at it.

Henry VI, Part 1
Funeral of King Henry the 5th, Henry VI makes his approach to France. Henry VI fashions as thy lord protector.

Henry VI, Part 2

King Henry the 6th, where the Cardinal is seen mocking protectors with praise, as all the rage. Queen Margaret at King Henry VI, until the end.

Henry VI, Part 3

King Henry VI is busy fighting a succession of battles, France and England as having at it, yet again.

King Henry the 5th

King Henry 5 fight his way toward France, they reach the peaceful and loving responses of a French King.

Henry IV, Part 1

King Henry the 4th, from Palace to Pub, onto the battle fields again. Until there is no rebellion.

Henry IV, Part 2

Henry IV, from Palace, Priest and then tavern, he nevertheless finds some peace, after reflection. King Henry IV, and then King Henry V as fashionable by the end.

Titus Andronicus

A story of Romans and Goths, where roman sways give way. And then to see about Goths and proving worthiness.

28 Characters

Julius Caesar

Near the Final days of the 1st Caesar, and the continuation everlasting as through Octavius.

www.ingramcontent.com/pod-product-compliance
Lightning Source LLC
Chambersburg PA
CBHW071239080526
44587CB00013BA/1679